Chasing Home

For Grandmom
Who taught me my dreams were never too big

For Grandad
Who taught me the power of words

For Mom
Who taught me to love books

And for everyone else in this book
For being my people

Please be aware this book contains mention of grief, loss, car accidents, and medical trauma including prescription drugs and surgeries.

Foreword

I grew up in a small town in deep south Mississippi, about 45 minutes from the Mississippi River. Our house was surrounded by National Forest land and when cell phones came around we always lost service when we turned onto our road. I had a unique childhood in that my school was in town and I had a great social life, but when we made the 30-minute drive home we were checked out until the next time we went to town. Our neighborhood was also almost exclusively family. My Mom's parents lived next door and everyone else was probably a cousin somehow. Most days after school, if I didn't have band practice or piano lessons or horseback riding lessons, I'd walk over to Grandmom & Grandad's house and hang out with them for a few hours. I've always loved listening to my older family members tell their stories and reminisce on the past. Growing up the way I did fostered that appreciation. Listening to my Grandad's stories about being in the Navy, and my Dad's stories about exploring out West, and my Uncle Ronny's stories about traveling in his van and living in Mexico also fostered my sense of adventure and my craving to explore outside of the small town and our pocket of the Homochitto National Forest. How does one go from a band nerd living in a Mayberry-esque southern town to traveling the world? Not without learning a lot, and not without

sometimes doing it the hard way.

Origins

My family originally adopted Pensacola thanks to my Grandad and his time in the Navy. We lived in Mississippi instead thanks to his ancestors. He was a Scott from a very long line of Scotts, and his side of the family is a direct line of descendants of immigrants from the Scotland/Ireland area of the world. Specifically, we're descended from a group of people called the Picts who began immigrating to the US in the early 1600s. Originally, our ancestors were in the Carolinas, then trickled down to what is now Mississippi. After they arrived in Mississippi, the Scotts ended up obtaining a big chunk of land in Franklin County when the whole land grant deal was going on during the late 1800s, and a lot of those Scotts' descendants are still there. According to public records, it's called Pleasant Valley, but according to true locals, it's called Scott Holler (hollow). Grandad and his nine siblings all grew up on the family land in the post-Depression era, farming and plowing with the family mule and exploring the valley, which is fairly close to how I grew up on that same land about sixty years later.

Sometime in the 1950s, at the ripe old age of 18, Grandad left Scott Holler and joined the Navy to see the world. Fast forward a few years to the mid-1960s, and he'd met my Grandmom when they were both in college, married her, had a couple of kids, and was living in Pensacola because the Navy had sent them there for a few years. He and Grandmom bought a cute little house in Mallory Heights, a neighborhood I now have very fond memories of, and they proceeded to make lifelong friends while they fell in love with the Emerald Coast. Fast forward again to 1969 and Grandmom and Grandad just couldn't stay away from those friends and the emerald green waters and sugar sand beaches, even though the Navy had sent them elsewhere, so they started renting out the local lighthouse on the Navy base during the summers. This was back when you could rent half the living quarters for $2 a night. They did that for a couple of decades, then when the Navy stopped renting out the lighthouse, they started renting one of the cabins right down the road from the lighthouse multiple times a year. By the time I came along, we were spending pretty much every school holiday and most of the summers there. Those cabins on that stretch of sand on the Pensacola Sound overlooking the Pass are where my memories of Pensacola and my first idea of 'home' begins.

The Cabins

If I sit very still and close my eyes and take a deep breath, I can still smell the inside of those Navy base cabins. They smelled salty and damp, but with fresh ocean overtones; exactly the way you'd expect a beach cabin to smell. They had minimal but acceptable furniture, which now reminds me a lot of military base housing loaner furniture, and was usually made of some kind of sticky vinyl. The row of cabins was tucked away under some trees right on the water facing the westernmost point of Pensacola Beach. Even as a kid, they felt like our own private paradise.

My first memory of the cabins is not what you'd expect from a nice, relaxing beach trip. I was very young, probably around 2. I remember we had beached that day, and everyone was taking turns showering. Then we ate dinner, and after I finished I got bored, so I toddled into a bathroom and saw a shiny razor laying on the side of the tub. True to toddler form, I picked it up, and as if on purpose, ran my finger right down the blade. As soon as I saw the stream of blood that shortly followed the razor blade I screamed as loudly as my little lungs would allow and everyone came running into the bathroom. My dad scooped me up and ran cold water over my hand in the tiny bathroom sink, then he and Mom bandaged me up and sent me on my way. It was over as quickly as it had happened, but I still get a little dodgy around razors.

My second memory of the cabins is also a painful one. It's a wonder I love the ocean at all given our initial rocky start. It was peak summertime which meant we were living in our swimsuits and perpetually sandy. One morning, Mom put me in my blue bathing suit that had the neon-colored crab on the front and pom poms for bubbles (I loved squeezing water out of the pompoms), and she and Dad walked me down to the beach. We had been there a little while when I discovered a weird gelatinous blob that had washed up on the sand. I excitedly bent down and picked it up and started playing with it, noticing immediately how squishy it was. About the time I had sufficiently squished it all over my hands, the wind kicked up and blew sand directly into my eyes. Predictably, I dropped the blob (which was unfortunately a jellyfish) and immediately started rubbing my eyes *hard* to get all the sand out. I got the sand out, but also got the jellyfish in. After a few seconds my eyes felt like they had caught on fire. Mom and Dad had been watching me from where they sat under the umbrella, so I got about one good scream out before Dad snapped into emergency mode, jumped out of his chair, scooped me up, and ran to the cabin with me faster than Mom had ever seen him run. He went straight to the beer cooler, dug out a Coors Light, popped the top, and dumped it straight on my head.

This might seem like a party foul or questionable parenting at best, but at the time it was common knowledge that beer dissolved jellyfish 'stingers' and that rubbing it in would make it work better. Dad supplied the beer and I had the rubbing under control. Within a few seconds, I had sufficiently rubbed the beer into my eyes and had stopped screaming. Dad and I walked back down to the beach and I went back to playing in the sand. I didn't pick up any more blobs after that though.

Over the next few years, we went to the cabins countless times. Cousins came with us sometimes and the Mallory Heights Gang visited often. All of us loved the beach and most of the families had boats, so we spent a lot of time on or near or in the water together at all times of the day and night. One night, all the grown-ups decided we'd go crabbing. Mr. Wally Wakefield was the crabbing expert, so he started briefing everyone on how this event was going to go and telling us what to wear, making sure to tell us to wear tennis shoes into the water. I thought it was super weird to tell people to wear shoes into the water until he said something about the crabs pinching your toes. After that, I was PETRIFIED of crabs pinching my toes and it was all I could think about all night. I just bobbed alongside everyone when we went to gather the crabs, making very sure to keep my feet tucked as close to my body as I could. I don't remember if we got any crabs that night, but I most definitely did not get pinched. As of right now, I still haven't had any toes pinched by a crab, though I do let my feet touch the bottom quite a lot these days.

After about five years of spending every free weekend and holiday at the cabins, Grandmom and Grandad decided it was time to buy a house in Pensacola. The cabins, the first Pensacola house, and the Firestone house were not the only houses I grew up in, but when someone asks me where I'm from they come to mind first.

Fins

I can still feel the midday salt spray hitting me in the face and the sun on my skin, concentrated on my forearms and knees as I dangled my feet over the bow. I can hear the boat whooshing as it hits the surface of the water and smell the ocean as it fills up my nostrils at 18mph. It's been about twenty years, but I remember it as vividly as I remember what I did yesterday. We were out in the boat and had spent the whole day fishing (which means I had been sightseeing and reading my book on the bow while the boys fished and Mom drove the boat) and we had gone further down the beach than usual. On this particular day during this particular wild ocean event, we were trolling back home from Opal Beach.

Mom and Dad pulled in the fishing lines while the boat idled, and Ben and I were standing on either side of the center console, rocking with the gentle waves. I was staring longingly at the surface of the water, feeling like a piece of bread that's been toasting ALMOST too long and daydreaming about jumping in and cooling off as soon as the hooks were in the boat. That's when I saw it: a HUGE, dark fin came up out of the water about 10 feet from me, interrupting my refreshing daydream. It broke the surface, glided through the water for a few seconds, then gracefully sank back into the blue-green

water. It was black and rounded at the top, which is not typical for

sharks or dolphins, but since we were in the Emerald Coast waters

where pretty much every big fin is a shark or a dolphin, and since it

wasn't grey like the native bottlenose dolphins, my brain

immediately assumed it was a shark. I felt the adrenaline floodgates

burst open in my chest, and I instinctively yelled, "SHARK!!!" but

there was an echo from across the boat. Weirdly, Ben had yelled,

"SHARK!!" at almost the exact same time. I glanced over at him,

confused as Mom and Dad whipped their heads around, trying to

spot it. The mood on the boat immediately shifted from lazy, sun-

induced chill to suddenly excited and alert. Mom darted up to the

front of the boat where Ben and I were and watched the surface with

us. We all stared into the blue-green depths, anxiously waiting,

hoping to catch a glimpse of the huge fish. Within a minute, the fins

surfaced again. Then again. And again! Always in the same area, and

always <u>also on the other side of the boat.</u>

"Y'all? Are there _two sharks_?!" Mom asked incredulously as we

watched the fins on both sides of the boat sink below the surface for

the third time. After a few minutes, she moved to the back of the boat again to help Dad finish putting away the fishing gear as Ben and I kept staring into the water. I suddenly realized what was off about the fins, and the fourth time they broke the surface I knew those fins were definitely not sharks. They were too round, and they always moved in sync with one another. Slowly the idea that maybe they belonged to the same creature started to form in my brain. Around this time, Mom and Dad saw a huge tail come up about 15 feet behind the boat and started yelling, "NOT A SHARK!! NOT A SHARK!!" Ben and I snapped around and looked at them just in time to see a huge stingray tail glide back underneath the water.

All at once, we all realized what was happening. *There was a Giant Manta Ray flying underneath our boat.* Dad hurriedly leaned over the side to see if he could see any more of the huge creature and got a good view of the giant manta's big, black body as it dove back down to the cool, deep water. He stood back up and we all stood in a daze for a few minutes after that, letting what we'd seen take hold of our brains. After a few minutes the shock and excitement gave way to too much sun and we all geared up and jumped into the cool water, secretly hoping we'd see the Manta again.

Decades later, we all still remember that day very clearly because Giant Mantas just DON'T come to Pensacola. Not in the depth we were fishing in, anyway. It's too shallow and too hot and too crowded for such big animals. I don't think any of us really believed what we saw when it was happening, and I still can't really believe it. We don't tell the story often because it's just too crazy to be real. All of us have the same memories about it though, so it must have actually happened. In the summer of 2004ish, under the boiling hot sun, a giant manta ray with an estimated wingspan of 20 feet (!!!) flitted up under our little bitty boat in Pensacola, Florida in about 80 feet of water, and that's one of the moments during which the ocean violently stole my heart.

Boats

Until 2014, our family had Grandad's boat. It was an 18-foot McKee Craft, which is not large for a seafaring craft. Luckily, the Gulf of Mexico is docile compared to other large bodies of water on this planet, and the hull shape of the McKee Craft made it surprisingly sturdy. It was what I like to call it a flat v, but more professional boaters would call a round bottom v hull. This meant it had a standard, shallow v in the center and two rounded, shallower v's on the sides. When compared to a regular, single v bottom boat, our McKee Craft's hull style was much more stable. In other words, though she be but little (and somewhat rough riding), she is fierce when the waves get big and everyone is making a beeline towards home to try to outrun the Florida storms.

Grandad's boat was a center console with a flat, open bow that I could dangle my feet from. I did that as often as the grown-ups would let me and enjoyed many hours of inexplicable entertainment from feeling my feet dip into the water as we puttered along (at trolling speeds only) or floated in place. I could see all kinds of stuff from up there: jellyfish, dolphins playing with us, fish, rubble on the bottom on a good vis day.

My memories on the bow of Grandad's boat are all blended together now into one big string of sunsets on evenings when we'd spent the whole day out on the boat. Sometimes we were fishing, sometimes skiing or snorkeling, sometimes beaching in the places most beachgoers wouldn't want to make the trek to. Back in those days, we always launched out of Sherman Cove which was the marina on the naval base. Not the Sherman Cove that stands today. That one smells different and looks different and feels different thanks to Hurricane Ivan. My Sherman Cove is no longer with us, much like many of my favorite people.

My Sherman Cove consisted of a long, grey, weathered building, rickety docks, and a dusty, grey rock parking lot. It smelled like boat fuel and fish guts and brackish water and Coppertone sunscreen and diesel exhaust and sweaty dockhands. It was somewhat worse for wear having weathered several big storms, but to me it was beautiful. The epitome of a weathered Florida marina, it's the beginning and end of most of my favorite childhood memories. I can still remember rolling out of bed early in the morning and donning my swimsuit and boat shoes, piling into whatever minivan we were using that day, and heading to the base. We'd go through the gate, the guard would salute Grandad, and we'd drive to the marina. Often it would be pretty early in the morning, so the sun would have that gentle brightness to it. As we loaded the boat with our coolers and gear, it would softly but urgently kiss my skin as though to say, "Welcome back. It's time to have an adventure!" The water would be gently tapping the sides of the boats tied to the docks and I could almost hear it saying, *"let's go, let's go!"* over and over as I crossed the parking lot.

I'd walk out onto the docks; the old, rickety, wooden docks that rocked precariously when you walked on them, and trot carefully to the boat. We'd load up the rods and reels, the boat toys, the snorkel gear, the snacks, and the sunscreen. Grandad would get the motor running, everyone would pile in, and I'd hop onto the bow and dangle my feet over the edge as we idled out to the Pass. Then we'd spend a day in my own personal Heaven.

When it was time to go home from our fishing spots or snorkel reefs or 'secret beaches' after a day spent out in the Gulf, we had to come back into the Sound through the Pass and take a left at Sand

Island, which would point us due West. I can still feel the boat

clipping through the waves as we made that turn and headed

directly into all of those sunsets. The wind kissing my cheeks and

tousling my hair as pinks, golds, purples, reds, oranges, blues, and

sometimes some faint greens when the sunbeams mixed into the sky

just right, plastered the sky like a gigantic overhead mural. I'd be

sitting on the bow, with any combination of Mom, Dad, Grandmom,

Grandad, Ben, and Uncle Ronny in the boat behind me. I always

reveled in dipping my feet into the water when the boat sank deeper

into the water after a gentle wave and watched for sea critters in the

water as we clipped by. Even though those sunsets marked the end

of our day, they always felt like the beginning of something. I've

seen thousands of breathtaking sunsets since then, but the ones from

the bow of that McKee Craft will always be my favorites.

These days, Sherman Cove is still a marina with a boat launch and

a building, but the building is not on the water anymore. It's further

up in the parking lot and close to the road, separated from the docks

and the brackish water by a hot, concrete parking lot. It's comprised

of a couple of beige metal buildings, which is a harsh juxtaposition

with the softened, grey wood in my memories. Ivan ripped out a lot of the pine trees and the grey rocks have long since been paved over. The rickety boards on the docks have been fixed and don't wobble anymore, and there's hardly ever a parking spot. Hurricane Ivan wiped out almost all the best stuff I remember at Sherman Cove, and time took care of the rest. We even have a new boat that we still launch there sometimes. Even though so much has changed, once we get out into the inlet and turn toward the Pass, the years melt away and I'm 9 years old again, dangling my feet over the bow while we speed toward our secret beach. Time marches on, but the memories do too.

I am ten years old and my brother is five. He is at home with Grandmom, but Grandad brought me with him today and it makes me feel special. We're at Sherman Cove. He's sitting at one of the picnic tables with a group of men talking about things I don't understand. I'm wandering around looking at all the old boats and loving the smell of the brackish water and weathered wood and fish. I walk past the boats and wander to the end of the dock. It's quiet out here, except for the rhythmic plops of the boats in the water. I sit down and dangle my feet over the edge and take a deep breath.

"Ahhh," I think to myself, "I could nap here."

"SQUAWK!!!" I jump and look to my left. Pete the Pelican has arrived, and he's apparently decided to announce himself.

"Hey, Pete. How's it goin'?" I ask.

"SQUAWWWWWWWK!!" he yells, clearly telling me it'd be better if I had fish to give him. He should know better. I'm not the fisher in the family. He settles in on a piling close by and quickly drifts off into a light nap. I watch the minnows darting below my feet, snacking on things too small for me to see.

After a little while, my butt gets tired of sitting on the rough dock and I hop up and start toward the marina. Pete squawks a goodbye at me, and I wave back to him. When I get to Grandad he says, "Ready to go?"

"Sure," I say because I'm hot and hungry, but I doubt I'll ever really be

ready to leave. He stretches out one of his calloused hands and I reach up to

take it. As he closes his hand around mine I wake up.

Houses

After a few years of renting the cabins, everyone accepted that Pensacola was a permanent part of our lives and Grandmom and Grandad bought a house around the corner from the strip of beach all this started on. It was in a cute little subdivision that is now full of military families since it's walking distance from the back gate. That house was the first time I'd ever lived in a real-life neighborhood with cul-de-sacs and neighbors whose houses were six feet from yours and parks and bike trails and multiple kids my own age. All of the streets were named for nautical terms, and our house was on a cul-de-sac toward the back of the neighborhood.

We had a lot of fun in that house in the cul-de-sac. Ben and I got to trick-or-treat and get candy at <u>so</u> many houses. We made friends with our neighbors, and friends and family visited a lot. My best friend Hannah and I got our first terrible sunburns the summer we were eleven, and we spent a couple of days taking advantage of the cold tiles just inside the front door. We made a lot of happy memories in that house, and after a few years I had a connection to it I'd never had to a house before. The house, and Pensacola as a whole, had started to feel a little bit like home.

The Capstan Court house was our Pensacola hub for a few years, then in 2004, Grandmom got sick of living 45 minutes across town from all of her friends and she and Grandad bought a house in Cordova Park. They closed on the purchase of the new house and hadn't quite closed on the sale of the old one when disaster struck. Literally.

In early September 2004 Grandmom & Grandad were in the middle of selling the old house when the weather channels started talking about a huge hurricane developing in the Atlantic. As is often the case with hurricanes, the path predictions varied and weren't dependable until it was fairly close to landfall. By about the 10th though, it was clear Pensacola would be hit pretty hard. All of the adults had started to get nervous, and I could tell Grandad was particularly stressed. I didn't appreciate it then, but now I can't imagine how stressful it would be owning two homes in a town with a massive hurricane plowing straight for it. The weather channels kept saying things like "record-breaking" and "worst storm in living history" and I was worried our beaches would never be the same.

Then on September 16th at almost 2 in the morning, Hurricane Ivan slammed into Pensacola with a force nobody alive had ever seen. We were in Mississippi since school was supposed to be starting, and it was devastating to watch the news coverage. Most hurricanes that got news attention were scary, but you could always tell in the footage that the towns would generally be okay. This one was different. For days, nobody could get in or out of the city or off of Santa Rosa Island. Cell towers had been destroyed so nobody was able to check in with friends or family. The national guard deployed to the area and after that crews started clearing roadways pretty quickly, so after a few days of no real information we started getting updates from every news outlet in the country.

It was totally surreal. They'd play a blip of a street sign and I'd recognize the intersection but what I saw on the screen looked nothing like what I was used to seeing in real life. I vividly remember the first few looks we got at the beaches and I remember the dropping feeling in my stomach when I saw that several thirty-story condo buildings had been shoved off of their foundations. Other buildings had vanished completely and the roads were destroyed. At some point, a helicopter crew took an aerial shot flying down the length of the island and it was totally unrecognizable. I knew where the landmarks should be for our favorite beaches and the seafood restaurant everybody loved and where the touristy section melts into houses, but I couldn't pick any of that out of the footage playing on the screen.

At landfall, Hurricane Ivan was a category 3 storm with 120mph sustained winds and a maximum storm surge of 15ft. The locals who stayed say that between the wind and the water there was nowhere to hide, which was evident in the aftermath. Every bridge had major damage, parking lots and roads and homes were submerged for days after landfall, hot tubs and sofas and whole lives worth of stuff washed up on the shores of Gulf Breeze from the homes on the beach. Across the two-lane highway from our house near the cabins, an entire neighborhood was decimated. A whole subdivision of two-story homes had been wiped completely off of their foundations into the sea, leaving nothing but concrete slabs behind. Our local friends were devastated and sure the beach would never be the same. Thankfully, though they were right and the landscape was permanently changed, we've been able to see it return to a thriving vacation spot with many of the things we lost to Ivan being replaced.

Somehow, in the midst of all of that disaster, between BOTH houses Grandmom and Grandad owned at the time of landfall, we only lost a few shingles. I remember the day Mom and Dad loaded up to go with Grandmom and Grandad to check on the houses. They packed the cars like they usually did for Pensacola trips, then they loaded up the flatbed trailer with barrels of water and gas. The news had been stressing to everyone that with so much destruction, clean water was scarce and gas was non-existent, so they opted to be prepared. I desperately wanted to go see my beaches and help, but Mom and Dad knew better. Ben and I stayed behind with some cousins and waited to hear the stories when everybody came home.

Our houses were fine, and most of our friends' homes were okay too. This was mostly thanks to the neighborhoods we lived in being at a higher elevation than a lot of the city. Grandad and Dad and Grandmom's brother, Uncle Ronny, wasted no time clearing tree parts and debris from both yards and replacing the missing shingles. We were lucky to have so little damage. The city as a whole was not. After they got home, Mom told us the National Guard was armed and out in full force all over town because gas and water were so valuable, they had become worth killing for to some people. When

Mom and Dad pulled into town with their trailer loaded with barrels

of the valuable resources, they were given an armed escort to the

house and warned to be wary. Due to the sheer quantity of structure

loss, the houseless population had also skyrocketed overnight. It felt

like more people were sleeping outside than not, looting was

rampant, roads were hazardous or closed, and the beach was as

unrecognizable in person as it had been on tv.

The next time I went to Pensacola, things were looking a smidge

better. It was December, so it had been about three months since

Ivan had hit. The bridges were still under repairs and had those

giant metal grates stretched across the washed-out spans. I can still

hear the MMMEEEERRRRRRRMMMMMM noise they made as we

drove over them. The beach still looked like a war zone, but more

like a war zone that bulldozers had started cleaning up. There were

pieces of people's lives, like hot tubs and beds and framed photos

and nightgowns, hanging amongst the trees and washed up into the

shorelines. Even boats were perched in treetops and washed up on

the beaches. Piles of rubble lined the streets and I was heartbroken.

We didn't have a lot of disastrous weather in Mississippi, so this was the first time I'd really experienced a force of nature causing

irreparable damage to something I loved.

I think some things in life are big enough they wake up a section

of your brain, and Ivan definitely woke up part of mine. Over the

next year or so, Pensacola worked together to put the pieces back

together and now, more than 25 years later, most people can't see the

scars the storm left behind. Ivan showed me how fragile the things

we love can be, and I realized that what I loved most was those

sugar sand beaches and the ocean that kissed them. That was the

first time I consciously realized that though I loved Mississippi and

the people we had there, it was Pensacola that was home.

The wind is howling around me. My hair is swirling across my face and I can barely stand up straight. Rain is pelting my skin and debris is flying through the air. The top of a tree, the neighbor's hot tub, a boat. They swirl in front of me and are thrown into the tree line across the road. I'm standing on the beach facing the Sound watching the destruction unfold. To my left, condos are collapsing. I'm secretly thrilled because even though those condos bring in tourist dollars, they make the skyline ugly, and they damage the nature around them. To my right, dunes are being flattened and my heart is breaking. Storms are a part of nature, and so is the havoc they wreak, but this is my home and it's being decimated before my eyes. I look up into the sky and I can't believe my eyes. Above my head, the giant manta ray, a pod of dolphins, and the fish from the coral reef are being tossed around in the wind like misplaced ragdolls. I scream into the wind, "No! We need them!" The wind does not listen. They are thrown into the tree line amongst the hot tubs and boats. I collapse into panicked sobs on the sand. My water-dwelling friends' bodies are a sick background to the rising water level and I don't care enough to move. As the storm surge covers my face, I awaken.

Christmases

Once we were on the other side of town, we were close to everybody we'd been missing for the last few years and I was finally getting to spend a lot of time with Grandmom's friends, Patti, Em, and Mary. All of them were always doing something or going somewhere together and I immediately gravitated toward them. Grandmom was a born hostess, so the new house turned into a central location for visiting, late night Dominoes games, out of town visitors and parties.

My favorite parties were the annual Beignet Parties we had every year on Christmas Eve. Grandad's sisters, Aunt Winnie and Aunt Frances, would come with us from Mississippi and Grandmom's brother, Uncle Ronny, would drive over from San Destin. We'd all spend two weeks decorating the house, going light seeing, meeting up with local friends at Christmas parades and candlelight services, and prepping for Beignet Party Day. Grandad claimed he bummed the original Café du Monde beignet recipe off some chef in the Navy at some point during his active-duty days and he'd start prepping the dough weeks in advance.

First, he'd spend half a day getting the dough prepared and put it into tall, rectangular Tupperware containers so it could rise until party day. Every day between then and the party, he'd take the dough out, knead it thoroughly, then put it back in its Tupperware. The night before the party we'd get all the Christmas dishes out and prepare the drink dispensers for cocoa and spiced tea and put the finishing touches on the decorations. On party day, we'd all get up at 4ish in the morning, Ben and I would don our Christmas aprons, and we'd all help Grandad get the dough and the frying oil ready for the day. Once that was all prepped, he'd start frying up hundreds of light, fluffy beignets. Ben helped him fry them then passed them to me across the kitchen where I was ready to coat them all in powdered sugar, then deliver them to the guests in the living room and sunporch. At any given party, we averaged about 50 guests, mostly Grandmom and Grandad's friends from the Navy days and their families. They'd start arriving around five thirty in the morning and drift in and out until around ten, visiting and catching up and gawking over the main attraction (second to the beignets), the Christmas Village.

Grandmom's Christmas Village was a big, beautiful display of an idyllic, snowy village at Christmastime all in miniature, sprawled over several long folding tables and sometimes the top of the hot tub that occupied a corner of the sunporch. Before the party guests could come enjoy the atmosphere it provided, we all had to set it up. It inevitably turned into a huge ordeal to meticulously wire and arrange about 50 houses, some mountains, around 200 trees, a street, and maybe 10 tiny people every Thanksgiving. Usually, Ben and I would do the unpacking of all of the pieces and arrange them on the tables, and Uncle Ronny would crawl around under the tables making sure all the cords were plugged into power strips in a way that wouldn't overload any outlets or burn the house down. There was always some kind of spat and everybody always resented the whole process. At least until the sun went down and we flipped the switch and all the houses glowed and the music played and the tiny people ice skated on their tiny icy pond. One year, Uncle Ronny even hand-built a huge, mountainside lake to go with it. It was truly magical, and I always wished I could go there for a day or two.

One year, during Christmas Village set up, Mrs. Em and her granddaughter, Brittany, came over to watch and offer moral support. Inevitably, Brittany got roped into helping, and a few hours later she and Ben and I were entirely fed up with the whole village and everyone around us. We were also *starving.* As if he could read

our minds, Grandad chose that time to quietly walk out onto the

porch and discreetly ask Ben if he wanted to go get lunch at the

drive-in down the street. Grandad went there every day for lunch,

but it was a treat for us kids. Grandad walked out of the sunporch,

then a few minutes later Ben did too. I had my phone in my pocket

and immediately after Ben disappeared into the house, I felt it

vibrate. It was a text from Ben.

Ben: 'Hey. Come with us to Jerry's. Bring Brittany but don't tell

anybody else. Be discreet.'

I shoved my phone back in my pocket and pretended to

straighten the fake snow as I made my way to where Brittany was

wrestling a tiny village human to try to get them to stay standing.

When I got to her I slipped my phone back out, showed her his text,

then calmly and quietly turned and left the sunporch. Before I got

into Grandad's van Brittany was right behind me. About thirty

minutes later, we were elbow deep in drive-in burgers and seafood

sandwiches, feeling not an ounce of guilt. When we finally got back

to the house Uncle Ronny had finished wiring the houses and once he got over having been abandoned halfway through, everyone thought it was pretty funny that the four of us had successfully snuck out for a lunch break. Naturally, we finished the rest of the set up in record time, working much better with full bellies and clear heads.

Christmas at The Florida House, as we called it, was always full of love and laughing and way too many presents. It was always too cold to beach, and often rainy, so we took advantage of the 'bad' weather and spent many a rainy or chilly day at the Naval Aviation Museum or the movie theater or going to the neighborhood park to play basketball and ride bikes. Ben and I had given up on Santa several years prior to our Florida Christmases becoming tradition which simplified things for Mom and Dad. Our Christmas vacations became just that: simple.

We'd always get the tree down after Thanksgiving (before the village pieces) and decorate it as a family with family heirloom ornaments and ornaments from Disney vacations and Grandmom's collection of White House ornaments. Before the year Grandmom finally got a pre-lit tree, we'd all spend the first hour trying to help

Uncle Ronny string the lights on the tree every year before we finally just gave up and let him do it. He's particular about things like that and it always looked better when we let him do it anyway. A couple of years in a row, Grandmom decided she wanted the front bushes lit up too. It only took two seasons of arguing over tangled lights in the front yard before we all unanimously decided that lit landscaping was a Christmas tradition we didn't really need to start. The decorations that made it up never really mattered as much as the people who were decorating. I loved decorating days because we were all together, setting the scene for the magic to come. Grandmom usually put her Rat Pack Christmas CD in the CD player to set the mood, and to this day I listen to the Rat Pack Christmas album pretty much on repeat from Thanksgiving to December 26th every year.

Nothing beats the magic of waking up on Christmas morning and believing deep down in your little kid heart that a big magic man brought you presents just for being good and that your family bought you EVEN MORE presents and that you'd spend the day playing with your new stuff with your family and fall asleep full of good food and good fun and good love, but those Pensacola

Christmases just might be tied for first. They were the perfect bridge

from full-on Christmas kid magic to the adult version.

Horses

The ocean is my best love, but horses were my first love. While the Giant Manta and the sunsets and the sunshine were stealing my heart, I was also head over heels for horseback riding. Mom started me out young, getting me into lessons when I was seven years old. By the time I was in second grade, I was saddling, bridling, riding, untacking, bathing, and feeding my very own leaser horse, Lucky. We leased Lucky from a local barn owned and operated by a powerhouse of a woman named Ms. Linda. She was in her forties with short, blonde-grey hair and sun-tanned skin. She could switch instantaneously from calm, gentle guidance with the student struggling to remember how to cinch a girth (the strap that holds a saddle on) to yelling across the entire property at someone who was misbehaving in the arena. Most importantly, she encouraged all of her students to live by a code of integrity, kindness, and asserting our worth, be it over a stubborn horse or our own lack of self-confidence or some snobby man telling us we couldn't run the barrels because we were girls.

I owned 5 horses during my horse girl days, and I learned a lot from all of them. The first was Tigger, and after I got him Mom and

Dad built a small barn at our house and fenced in some pasture area so I could ride him whenever I wanted, but they'd be nearby in case I got hurt. Tigger was a copper-colored Welsh Pony with a draft horse sized attitude. He liked to kick up his heels and throw me off every time I rode him so he could snack on the foliage around us. He was pushy and mean and gluttonous, but I loved him, and he gave me a crash course in how to stay on horses that don't want to be ridden and general horse care. The next horse I got was a spunky little Morgan horse who didn't like to respect personal space but loved to run. He was a warm, chocolate brown color with a black mane and tail, and he had one white foot and a broad white stripe all the way down his face. He was aptly named Renegade when we bought him, but Mom and I had soft hearts and quickly renamed him Moses. The irony of that name change wasn't something I'd see until years later, but he was definitely more Renegade than Moses.

Next, we got the three girls. Shelley was a copper-colored mare with a thin white stripe on her nose. She was a seasoned quarter horse whose left hip popped most of the time, but she could slow trot like a dream, and she was bulletproof (not scared of anything). This made her perfect for our trail rides around the house. Next we had Dusty, a solid black Tennessee Walking Horse I bought from my friend Jake. She thought she was a giant lap dog who loved her people and came running when we showed up at the barn. Dusty would do anything I asked her to, and we spent many an afternoon galloping up and down the creek and napping in the pasture together. Last but not least was Nutmeg, also a Tennessee Walking Horse, but decidedly NOT a lap dog. She was colored more like Shelley, but where Shelley was solid and tank-like, Nutmeg was flighty and lanky. She was high strung and every ride was a challenge, but by that point I appreciated being pushed to learn and grow in my understanding of horses so I loved her too.

The lessons I learned from Ms. Linda and the horses shaped the person I grew up to be and have helped guide me through a variety of speed bumps in life, in and out of the barn. One of the most important things she taught me was perseverance. More specifically, she taught us to always persevere, but to also learn when you needed a break or adjust your goals. I remember very vividly the day this lesson really took root in my brain.

It was a crisp, fall afternoon and I was the only one riding that day. I was trying to turn Moses into a Western Pleasure horse, which meant he'd need to learn to move smoothly from a walk, to a trot, to a canter, and to do lead changes and to hold his head at a certain height and to stop on a dime. Unsurprisingly, he wasn't having it. In hindsight, he was clearly wired to be a cow pony, doing things that allowed him to be quick on his feet and didn't require perfect form, but I was a Western Pleasure kid, so he needed to learn to be a Western Pleasure horse. On this day in particular he was feistier than usual and not at all interested in being ridden in the first place. I got him saddled and down to the arena, mounted up, and started trotting him around the sandy circle furthest from the barn, but every single time circle by the gate, he'd drift toward it, blatantly ignoring my direction and irritating me more and more with each pass. After about ten wonky circles, Ms. Linda saw what was happening from the barn and walked down the hill to come help. When she got to the arena, she could sense how frustrated I was getting, so she calmly and very matter-of-factly said, "You can cut your circles in half and only circle him at the other end of the arena so he doesn't notice the gate. Forget trying to make any big adjustments for him today. When he quits fighting, you've won, and you can both be done." Then she walked away.

Duh. Moving our circles away from the gate made perfect sense after she pointed it out, but I'd gotten so focused on forcing him to listen to me I'd lost sight of other solutions. I'd also forgotten completely that I was allowed to adjust the goal if the original plan went sideways, and I was relieved that she'd reminded me of that. I immediately cut our circles in half, so we only used the end of the arena furthest from the gate. It didn't fix the issue entirely, but I trusted Ms. Linda and didn't quit. I rode that horse in tiny little circles for what felt like an eternity, and EVERY time we'd circle back closest to the gate, he'd do something jerkish, like kick his heels up in a little buck, or swerve just enough to be annoying before skipping right back over to where he was supposed to be or toss his head and try to take control of the reins. Still, I kept pushing. Every ten or so circles, we'd change direction which put the gate on the opposite side of his body when we passed it, mostly to keep me from totally wearing out one side of my body but also to keep him from being able to plan ahead too much. Finally, as the sun started to really disappear below the horizon and my leg muscles started to cramp from constant correction, we went one full circle with no attitude. No bucking, no swerving, no tossing his head. Just a smooth, perfect circle all the way around. I knew better than to let myself get excited yet in case it was a fluke, so we did two more circles just to be sure. Success! No attitude! He'd finally decided to let me be in charge or gotten tired enough he didn't care anymore. Either way, it was a huge jump for us as a team, and that feeling was worth a zillion tiny little circles.

To reward both of us for the win, I let him do his favorite thing and we ran around the cloverleaf shaped barrel pattern before we went back to the barn. He loved being able to stretch his legs and spin around those barrels, and I loved the feeling of flying so it was a treat for both of us. After that day, he still occasionally protested being ridden, and sometimes even swerved toward the gate, but because I felt more confident that I could successfully correct him and because he knew I wouldn't quit, he only ever needed one correction to get back on track. As an adult, I've faced a lot of hard stuff, and often I've really wanted to quit. Whenever I feel like I just can't handle any more stress or grief or injustice, I remember that little brown cow pony and all those circles we did at the far end of the arena, and I just keep on trotting in my own tiny circles until the hard thing is over and I can run the barrels.

Spending time around horses in general teaches you very quickly that you can't cut corners, and that everything comes with hard stuff, even fun. During my horse years I had to learn to trim their hooves, bathe them, give them shots, worm them (shoot wormer down their throats with a huge syringe), help them give birth, castrate them, and constantly scoop their poop. I also had to learn to take care of saddles and saddle pads and halters and lead ropes and bridles and fences and horse trailers. Then when I started doing horse shows, I had to take care of my boots and my hat and my show clothes too. I've been kicked, bitten, thrown, and stepped on more times than I can count. I learned quickly that putting a horse in their stall still wet from a ride or a bath during the winter could kill them, that giving them too much of what we call sweet feed (food pellets soaked in molasses) could make them very sick, and that not cleaning out stalls properly could seriously damage their feet. Learning all of those things at such a young age was a very formative lesson, and it helped me develop a very deep seated and instinctive work ethic I don't think I'll ever be able to shake.

Probably my favorite thing I learned from growing up with

horses is animal psychology. I remember the first time I got to watch somebody start training a young horse. He was a beautiful black and white pinto, about a year old, and one hundred percent high strung male. The person training him was quite the opposite. She was middle aged, brunette, and so soft spoken I could barely hear her over the horse's snorts and whinnies. They were in a round pen, which is exactly what it sounds like, between the barn and arena at Ms. Linda's and watching the two of them was like watching an imbalanced ballet class. No matter what stunts he pulled trying to get away or assert himself over her, she never reacted or broke her focus. He'd kick his heels up and whinny as loud as he could, and she'd stay planted where she was. She'd move toward him with a blanket, which is the first step in teaching a horse to wear a saddle, and he'd panic. She'd stop and stay put until he calmed down, then take another step. Repeat. Repeat. Repeat. Until finally, she could approach him with the blanket. Then she'd do it all over again with touching him with the blanket, then again with rubbing it on his back and legs, then again with putting it on his back.

It took all day for her to get him to let her put that blanket on his back, which may sound tedious and boring to most people, but I was absolutely fascinated. I'd seen my fair share of bad horse trainers. The ones who thought horses were objects to be broken and conquered. This was different though. This process was all about working <u>with</u> the horse's instincts to teach them that things didn't have to be scary. After that day, I decided to learn everything I could about gentle training and to start treating my own horses that way. I noticed an immediate shift in the way Moses started reacting to me and behaving when we were working together, which fueled my hunger for learning about this new method even more. Mom and Dad bought me a book called Horses for Dummies, and later another book more specifically focused on what it called "the join-up method." Join-up took the gentle approach I'd observed in the round pen and bumped it to the next level. It was all about starting on the ground and the horse's feet and creating a bond based in respect and herd hierarchy, then building from that to a level of horse & rider connection I'd never seen before. I devoured the join-up book and still wanted more, and that's when Mom and Dad discovered Clinton Anderson.

Clinton is an Australian horse trainer known for his Downunder Horsemanship classes which are based in effectively communicating with horses. At the time we discovered him, he was still a fairly small name in the horse world, but he had a set of DVDs you could order to learn his method so that's what we did. I sat enraptured with Clinton and his horse as he started on the ground, using only his voice and a spinning lead rope to communicate with the horse about what he wanted. There was no force, no pain inflicted, no yelling or whips. It was calm, gentle, and geared specifically toward things the horse understood. Clinton also taught about learning to read a horse's body language so they could communicate to you, too. So if you were spinning your lead rope and asking your horse to move their hindquarters away from you, and they pinned their ears and clamped their tail down, you could know that maybe they weren't being indignant, maybe they were in pain and needed a vet visit or a rock plucked out of their shoe.

By the end of the set of DVDs Clinton could ride his horse with no saddle, bridle, or spurs and have him move from standing still to spinning in circles, or galloping, or moving at a slow walk or trot simply by using a little leg pressure and his voice. Then, he could get that spinning, galloping horse to stop *on a dime* by just shifting his seat and practically whispering a quick 'whoa.' I was hooked and dying to get to that point with my own horses. I had dreams at night

for weeks of riding Moses like Clinton rode his horse, at breakneck

speeds across the Australian Outback then with no visible or audible

cues, stopping so fast we kicked up a cloud of dust bigger than the

horse.

    I started implementing Clinton's groundwork methods with

Moses every time I took him out of the barn. Moses and I had always

butted heads, sometimes literally, and we frustrated each other often

because he usually just flat didn't want to do what I was telling him

to do. I was hopeful this new method would help with all of that

though, so I walked into the round pen on that first day optimistic.

At first he was resistant, unaccustomed to the spinning lead rope

and preferring to rub his huge head all over me instead of respecting

the space I asked him for. Eventually though, he started making

progress. He stopped pushing me around and rubbing his face on

me to get me out of his way, and he started giving into pressure

from the spinning rope and listening for my quiet verbal cues.

    After a few weeks, Moses and I had the groundwork down pat so

I decided to move to riding again. It was astounding to me how quickly he picked up on all of the new cues, and it felt like after all those tiny circles in the arena and all the headbutts and fights we'd had, we were finally understanding each other. It was incredible. After just a few sessions he'd stopped resisting me and I'd started learning what his specific behaviors were communicating to me. We were finally working together as a team and it felt like magic. I wholly adopted this new, intuitive way of interacting with horses, and eventually noticed I'd adapted it to work with all of the animals at the barn. What I didn't realize then was that it wasn't just with animals. This deeply psychological way of communicating with other living beings wholly shaped the way I interact with people too. It made my crappy customer service jobs easier but much more emotionally taxing. When Grandmom got sick, it made taking care of her a lot easier, especially when she struggled to talk. Now as an independent adult who exists in several marginalized spaces and participates actively in social justice causes, these concepts I initially took from a horse training video help me effectively navigate some of the most difficult kinds of people.

Nutmeg was another horse who taught me a lesson about animal psychology, just in a very different way. We bought her from a man who owned a chicken farm a couple of hours from us, and I'd known

the moment I laid eyes on her that we had to take her home with us.

She was filthy and so skinny I could count her ribs, and her head

hung low with exhaustion. Despite all of that, though, her eyes were

bright and she was gentle when I approached her. She let me ride

her, and I was delighted by how smooth she was. Thankfully Mom

and Dad saw the same things I did, and we drove her home that day.

After about two weeks of living with us, a sudsy bath, and

steadily eating a solid, healthy diet it became more clear to me why

she had been starved at her prior home. She was <u>extremely</u>

energetic, and the more filled out she got, the more wildly she

behaved. She was well trained and friendly, but she didn't like

standing still to be saddled, or groomed, or to have her feet trimmed.

She was always ready to go go go and would start trotting almost

before my butt hit the saddle, ready to fly. While I loved that because

I love riding fast horses, we quickly decided she wasn't going to be

the horse we let guests ride. She was just for me, and I was secretly

very okay with that.

One thing I desperately wanted to do was ride her bareback. I loved the connection that came with bareback riding, and I'd advanced to a stage in my riding where I didn't really need the saddle for balance anymore, so I rode bareback as often as I could and rarely put a saddle on Dusty or Shelley. Mom cautioned me against riding Nutmeg bareback though, and she had good points. Nutmeg was much faster than the other two girls, and she was less predictable. She'd be a lot harder to stick to, and she also liked to start moving as I was climbing onto her which would be dangerous if there was no saddle to hold me onto her.

So for months and months, I only rode Nutmeg with a saddle on her. I played by the rules and nobody got hurt, but I still wanted to try riding her bareback *really bad*. She was a very intuitive horse and the Clinton Anderson methods I'd perfected with Moses worked like an absolute dream with her. We'd gotten so good at communicating I didn't even need to hold her lead rope to walk her places. She just followed me wherever I went as soon as I clipped it to her halter. She'd also gotten really, really good at tuning into my cues when we went out riding. I rarely had to put any pressure on the reins. All I had to do was shift my position in the saddle and use gentle leg pressure and she did exactly what I asked. I soft tap from my left leg? She spun to the right. If I sat back a little more in the saddle? She'd stop on a dime. A gentle squeeze from both legs? Off she'd go until the next cue. She was fantastic, but I knew that riding bareback made all of those cues so much easier to pick up on and I couldn't stop wondering just how good it could get for her if there was no saddle impeding our communication.

One Saturday morning in the Spring semester of my junior year in high school, I woke up and decided I wanted to hang out with Nutmeg. I drove our Polaris Ranger from our house to the barn and got her out of the pasture, then tied her up so I could groom her. I gave her a good combing and cleaned out her feet and brushed out her mane and tail until they shone. Then I walked her to the round pen and we started the groundwork routine we'd nearly perfected. The goal was for her to accept me as the 'herd leader' and to tune in to all of my body language so I didn't need any ropes or verbal cues to tell her what I wanted. She'd gotten really good at all of that, but she was easily distracted so it didn't always last very long. Today though, I could feel that something was different. We walked into the round pen, I took her halter and lead rope off, and she immediately started trotting in circles. I angled myself so my body lined up with her hindquarters and took a step closer and she immediately moved into a canter. After a few circles, I took several steps back and she slowed to a walk. I stepped closer and she skipped back into a trot, then I took two steps back and turned my back to her and waited. Immediately I heard her slow to a walk, then start approaching. She walked across the round pen until she was about a foot behind me, stopped, and started licking her lips, signaling that she was paying attention to only me and she was ready to do what I asked. I grinned and turned to scratch her ears. The exercise had gone perfectly, and I heard a voice in my head that said, "If you're ever going to ride her bareback, this is the day." I knew it was right.

I put the halter back on her and draped the lead over her neck, knowing I wouldn't need it, then she followed me as I walked back over to the barn. I tied her to our saddling tie so she wouldn't follow me while I found what I needed, then I started looking for a stool. Nutmeg was pretty tall at 16 hands (the way we measure horses; one hand is about four inches, so she was 5' 3" at the top of her back), and I'm pretty short at 5'3" so I knew I wouldn't be able to get on her without some help. I searched the whole barn for about twenty minutes before I decided I wouldn't find an actual stool and I'd have to improvise. I looked around and spotted two feed buckets sitting next to the feed room door. *Aha!* I grabbed them and walked back over to Nutmeg. I untied her from the saddling tie, knowing I wouldn't be able to reach it once I got on her, stacked the buckets up next to her, and stepped on top of them full of confidence.

One thing about Nutmeg I'd conveniently forgotten about on this day was that certain loud noises scared her. Specifically, loud crashing noises. Which is exactly the kind of noise the buckets made as I shoved off of them and threw my leg over her back. I had just managed to grab ahold of her neck with my arms and wrap my legs around her belly when the buckets fell and she took off like she was breaking out of a gate at the Kentucky Derby. She was running down the driveway at full speed and I was hanging off the side of her like the Native Americans used to do in those old western movies, and after a few seconds I realized I was actually in danger. The way I saw it there were three possible outcomes: I could hang there until my arms got tired and then let myself fall and hope I didn't get trampled, I could hang there until Nutmeg inevitably raked me off on a tree or a light pole which would probably result in my neck being broken and my skull being crushed, or I could shove myself backward away from her and hope for the best. I opted for the latter. The last thing I remember is releasing my hold on her neck and belly and shoving my body away from her as hard as I could, then everything went black.

I still don't know how long I laid in our gravel driveway before I came to, but when I did Nutmeg was pacing back and forth along the fence line losing her mind and trying to get back to her herd (Shelley and Dusty) and my head was absolutely pounding. I knew immediately that I had a concussion, and I started doing a mental body scan to see if I had any other injuries. Arms, hands, torso, all good. Right leg, all good. Left leg, al- oh. Oh no. My left shin felt like it was probably broken. I took a deep breath and wiggled my toes. They were fine but the movement made my shin feel like it was on fire, so I stopped quickly. Then I reached for the walkie talkie I always had with me when I was with the horses and I called for Mom and Dad to come help me.

beepbeep "Mom, Dad? I need some help. I think I'm okay, but I fell off Nutmeg and I don't want to move in case I'm more hurt than I realize." *beepbeep*

A few seconds passed, then,

beepbeep "Okay stay there. We're on the way." *beepbeep*

It was Mom's voice, but I'd heard Dad shuffling around in the background, probably grabbing his truck keys. Within five minutes they were coming down the driveway. They got to where I was still lying in the gravel and both jumped out of the truck, Mom making a beeline for Nutmeg (she's not great with blood so this was definitely the best task for her to choose) and Dad coming straight to me. Mom settled Nutmeg down and got her back into the pasture while Dad checked me out and decided other than being "clearly concussed," I was fine, and that my leg was just bruised, not broken.

"What do you mean, clearly concussed?" I asked him, mildly insulted.

He paused for a second, then said, "Oh. You haven't seen it. Hang on."

He trotted to his truck, grabbed something, and came back over and held it out to me. It was a handheld mirror, so I held it up and looked at myself in the reflection.

Holy shit, I thought upon seeing my forehead. It was covered in deep purple bruises that looked very much like the pattern a gravel driveway might look like if it was stamped onto skin. That was when I realized what had happened. When I shoved myself away from Nutmeg's body, her back hoof had caught the back of my head and kicked it into the driveway, which immediately knocked me unconscious, gave me a concussion, and resulted in the bruises spreading across my forehead. I looked at Dad and said, "Oh. I get it now," and we both laughed. I stopped almost immediately because laughing *hurt*, then he helped me slowly stand up and get in the truck. Mom had gotten the girls settled and fed for the night, so we all loaded up and went home where Dad snapped smoothly into doctor mode and I spent the next several days doing very little.

That whole incident taught me a very valuable lesson I've always been thankful for; don't let one good day erase a clear pattern. Just because Nutmeg had been an angel in the round pen didn't mean her personality had been altered, she'd just had a good day. This lesson has helped me confidently identify and walk away from people who are toxic or just not people who belong in my life, even if they have a good day and seem like they might change. Cheating boyfriends? Goodbye. Manipulative friends? Blocked. Terrible jobs and bosses? No thanks. No matter how many times I've heard "but I swear I'll be better now" or "I'm sorry, just give me a second chance" I just remember lying in the driveway with big, purple bruises tattooed across my forehead and I very thankfully remove those people or circumstances from my life. Did I need a concussion to learn that? Maybe not. But I'm very glad I got the lesson.

Shortly after the 'getting my head kicked' incident, Mom and Dad decided three horses was a lot and that Nutmeg might be better suited for a hyper kid who loved doing speed events in horse shows. They were right and I knew I'd be headed to college in the next few years anyway, so we decided to sell her, and she was bought by a couple for their hyper kid who loved doing speed events in horse shows. I got to see her in a horse show a few months later and she looked amazing, zipping in and out of the line of poles in the middle of the arena, mane and tail flying in the wind, and I knew we'd made the right call.

Soon after Nutmeg found her new home, the subject of me leaving for college officially arose. I knew I'd be going to the community college about thirty minutes away before transferring to a university, so I'd be home most weekends, but taking care of horses is a lot of work, even if it's just five days a week. Mom and Dad understandably didn't want to take over that responsibility for me and we discussed the girls would need new homes before I left, so I decided to enjoy the year we had left together as much as I could.

A few months later, we moved Shelley to Ms. Linda's barn and shortly after that she was bought by a nice family with a daughter who wanted to start doing horse shows. It was sad, but planned, and I knew she would be happy with her new humans. Plus, I still had Dusty and she and I were closest out of the three girls anyway. I knew we'd just enjoy our last few months together in peace, then I'd find her a good home the summer before I left for school.

One Wednesday a few weeks later, I got the call that someone was buying Dusty. I left church early and drove home, crying the whole way. I went straight to the barn and was relieved to see I was the first one there. Before the car was settled in park, I jumped out, put Dusty's bridle on her, hopped on bareback, and we went for one last ride around the valley. I cherished the way she leaned into my commands and how smoothly we worked together. I soaked up the way it felt to fly with her across the pastures and the way her mane tickled my arm as it flowed in the wind. It often felt like she did things before I finished thinking about telling her to and I loved that connection we had.

We spent about a half hour just existing together, me telling her how much I loved her and what a good girl she was and how thankful I was for her. She'd been a steady presence for me for years, always running to the barn when I got there just to spend time with me, letting me cry into her neck when things felt hard, and making me laugh with her goofy antics. I rode her to the highest point on the property and watched the sun sink behind the trees, combing her mane with my fingers. After the sun disappeared, we slowly plodded home.

We got back to the barn as her new owners were pulling in with their trailer and Mom and Grandmom had just parked. I kissed Dusty on her soft, warm nose, breathed her in one last time, then switched her bridle out for her bright pink halter and lead rope. I'd always loved the way the bright colors popped against her black hair. I could feel my heart breaking as I handed her over to her new family. With that goodbye, all of my horses were gone, and my barn was empty for the first time in almost a decade. I stayed there for a while after Mom and Grandmom went home, and when I finally left, I knew my life had just changed in a big way.

I did get to ride again eventually. By the end of my first year of college I missed horses and the beach so badly I decided to move to Pensacola for the summer and find a job doing something with horses. A few weeks before finals, I started looking for a job and found a barn about thirty minutes from the Firestone house, so I called the number listed on the website. Voicemail. I left a message briefly explaining who I was and how long I'd been riding and what I was looking for then hung up and hoped for the best. Later that evening, the phone rang and my heart skipped a beat. I trotted over to it and picked it up.

"Hello?" I said.

"Hi, is this Rebecca? This is Sharon from the Horse Barn. I got your message earlier and I wanted to call and see if you still wanted a job." All of that was said in one quick breath by a voice that sounded like it sang in church every Sunday but also smoked during the week.

"Yes of course! I'm definitely still interested! What did you have in mind?" I asked excitedly.

Cheryl told me she needed somebody to help her and her daughter lead trail rides, keep the barn and the horses clean, and to be an instructor for the riding camps she'd have going for kids all summer. It sounded PERFECT, and as soon as she finished explaining the duties and pay to me, I emphatically accepted. She asked if I could start the first week of June and I couldn't believe I'd gotten so lucky. For the next few weeks, all I could think about was finally living my dream and spending the whole summer with horses *and* the beach. Finals flew by in a blur and before I knew it I was packing my biggest suitcase full of bathing suits, blue jeans, and boots and on my way to Florida. Then one day in the first week of June, I woke up at five in the morning, got dressed for riding all day, and drove out to the barn to meet the team and the horses I'd be spending the next two months hanging out with.

Cheryl was a short, sprightly woman with bright blonde hair and piercing blue eyes. She was immediately endearing, but I could tell she was not a person who took anyone's bullshit. I knew we'd get along. Her daughter, Shelby, was a few years younger than I was and had the same blue eyes as her mom, but the similarities stopped there. She was already taller than Cheryl and she had dark brown hair. She loved horses like her Mom did, but she had just graduated from high school and was getting ready to leave home. Her best friend, Angel, was tall and lanky with long brown hair and she also helped out a lot. I immediately liked all of them and after the introductions were done, we headed to the barn to meet the animals. An hour later I'd met all the horses, the barn cats, and the dogs on the property and I'd fallen in love with the whole circus.

I spent that summer getting to know the horses, taking them out on trail rides with clients, and teaching elementary aged kids how to ride. There were about fifteen horses in total, and generally they were all calm and well behaved. None of them had any behavioral issues outside of a few high-strung ones who just wanted to run every time we saddled them up. Then there was Frankie. Every horse is different, and all of them have their own little quirks. Some chew on walls, some buck if you kick them in the right (wrong?) spot, some will come running from across the pasture if they hear your car in the driveway, and some bite. A few bite at very specific times, like when you tighten the cinch strap that holds on the saddle. Frankie specifically loved to swing his head around and try to bite people at that precise moment when both of your hands are busy tightening the strap around his belly and you can't defend yourself.

I never rode Frankie because we just didn't jive, and I did happen to jive really well with another horse in the barn, so it made sense for me to not spend much one-on-one time with him. One day, though, I had a trail ride to lead and one of the clients sounded like a good match skill-wise for him, so I got him out of his stall and started saddling him up. If you've ever saddled a horse, you know you saddle them on their left side and you end up standing so that you're facing their torso and your left arm is closest to their head. That's how I was positioned when I grabbed the cinch strap with both hands and pulled straight up to tighten it, making sure to keep my left elbow elevated to keep Frankie from being able to bite any soft tissue. My efforts were in vain. Frankie swung his big, brown head around at warp speed as I tightened the cinch and closed his front teeth over a tiny piece of skin on the back of my arm. You know the spot. The one you pinch when your sibling has just pushed it TOO FAR and you need to knock them to their knees for a second. The one that makes you want to cry and hurts for hours after it's been pinched. Yeah, that one. Frankie's teeth clamped down right on that spot and suddenly I heard Ms. Linda in my head telling me another lesson she'd taught us and I'd filed away for a rainy day.

I don't remember when Ms. Linda told me this, but at some point during the 10ish years I rode at her barn, she told me that if a horse bites you, you have to bite it back. Specifically, you bite it on the ear. Allegedly, after that they'd never bite you again. I never asked for clarification or specifics because I'd heard this about dogs and babies too, but I filed that one away just in case I ever needed it. So when Frankie bit me, almost instinctively, I reached up and grabbed his ear, put it between my teeth, and bit down. It was a gentle bite. I didn't want to hurt him, just get his attention, so I was quick but careful not to bite too hard. However, as soon as I bit down, he jerked his head up, which jerked his ear out of my mouth between my left canines and shredded the tip of his ear. I jumped back and sputtered, spitting blood and horsehair out of my mouth, and Frankie screamed.

I'd never heard a horse scream before, but it made my blood curdle and the hair stand up on the back of my neck. He screamed and started tossing his head, as though he was trying to shake off a stinging insect. I started speaking softly to him and trying to calm him down so I could check his ear, but he wouldn't let me anywhere near his face or head. After a few minutes he stopped throwing his head around and I could see his ear was bleeding but still intact. I immediately called my boss/Frankie's owner and told her what had happened and she came down from the house to the barn to inspect the damage. Frankie wasn't too keen on her touching his face or head either, but if I stood where he could see me, he'd let her inspect him. Thankfully, she discovered his injury was entirely superficial, and even though Frankie had to be emotionally rehabilitated before he'd let people touch his head again, he never tried to bite anyone again after that.

I learned many lessons from horses growing up, probably a few I don't even realize I learned. I'm forever thankful to have had the opportunity to spend those years with them even if it did result in a few bumps, bruises, and scars. Horses taught me about other living creatures, and the ocean has taught me infinite things about myself. They are my two greatest loves, and I wouldn't be who I am today without their influences.

I'm riding Dusty and we're FLYING across the ground. There's no saddle, no bridle, but we don't need it today. She's in my head, and I'm in hers. She knows where I want to go before I really think it, and she knows today I want to R U N. We zip across the open field into an orchard, gleaming red apples flying by in a blood-colored blur. I'm desperate for open scenery and freedom. I've felt so hemmed up lately. Dusty agrees, and cuts through the trees onto a well-worn path.

"Where are you going?" I ask. I don't recognize this route.

"Just trust me, little one," she says in a soothing voice in my head. So I do. Within minutes we're on a wide beach. It's not Pensacola; the sand is firmer and easy for Dusty to run on. It's open, though, and when we're clear of the trees she kicks it into high gear. She gallops across the sandy expanse and I stretch my arms out wide, whooping with her in our new-found freedom. She laughs in my head and goes even faster, kicking up damp sand behind us.

Suddenly, she leaps into the air and we're flying just above the beach. I can feel her surprise, so I know this wasn't planned, but it's so much fun we don't bother thinking about it much. She zig-zags across the breaking waves, dipping her feet into them occasionally and neighing her joyous laughter into the sea spray. I blink and we're underwater, except it's not really us anymore. It is, but it isn't. She's still Dusty and she's still in my head, but now she's a huge, elegant whale shark and I'm a pelican perched on her back, somehow able to stay on. Her bright white spots sit atop her back with me and she's speeding through the water, chasing freedom just like she was doing on the beach. She breaches, flying high into the air and belly flopping back into the water with a huge SPLASH. I jump into the air and fly above her, swooping down to drag my toes in the water and soaring high with the wind. We cackle together at the ridiculousness of it all. I land on her back and suddenly I'm human again. I lean down and hug her wide, grey neck and she whinnies at me, whipping her tail back and forth and propelling us through the blue water.

BBBAAAHHH BBBAAAAHHH BBBAAAHHH BBBAAAHHH

My brother's alarm clock rips me back to reality and I sigh as I accept the end of my dream, longing for the freedom of the open ocean, wings, and a fast horse.

Wrecked

In September 2013 I was in college at a university about 2 hours from where we lived in Mississippi. One weekend, I decided to drive home and surprise Mom and Dad. When I got there, Mom was still at work so I said 'hi' to Dad, walked into my room, and dropped my suitcase on the floor. I remember the sharp clack sound the feet made when they hit the tile. The next sound I heard was Dad's first responder radio going off to let everyone know they needed assistance with a car accident on the highway. I wouldn't know for a few minutes after that how much that call would change my life, but in that moment I felt time slow down. It took years to speed up again.

Grandmom had over 30 broken bones and multiple contusions including seatbelt bruising, but our most pressing issue during the first few days in the ICU was fluid shift. This phenomenon occurs when a human body encounters a level of force so intense the cellular fluid is forced out of the individual cells through the cell membrane into the surrounding area. Medically, there's not much you can do except wait for the cells to absorb their fluid again (which apparently, they generally do). Non-medically, you look like the

Michelin Man until the reabsorption happens. So when I went in to see Grandmom in the Surgical ICU the morning after the accident, I walked in to see tubes and lines going everywhere, and my bruised, broken, intubated, Michelin Man of a grandmother buried underneath them. I remember thinking "man if this wasn't so scary it would be super funny." But it was scary, so it wasn't funny.

The next week or so is a blur. People visited. Lots of people visited. So many wonderful, kind, loving people came to see my sweet Grandmom. They hugged us and prayed with us and brought us supplies and provided breaks in the stress riddled monotony that we desperately needed. Her best friends who lived too far away to visit, Mrs. Patti and Ms. Em, called frequently for updates to pass along to the rest of her friends. Thoughts of life outside of the SICU floor vanished and our lives revolved around visiting hours and phone calls. When visitors weren't there, we had our ICU waiting room friends. Mom and I were camping out with 10-20 other people in there depending on the day, and everyone welcomed a chance to talk to people who weren't doctors and nurses.

One man's wife was a patient because she'd had a motorcycle

wreck and had a bad head injury. She desperately and exclusively

needed a blood transfusion, but they were Jehovah's Witnesses. The

day she died was the day I started to come out of my own shock a

little bit and connect more fully to what was happening around me.

Quickly, my old assumption that the world will take care of us

started disappearing. Another family was there because their kid

was in a four-wheeler accident. He didn't make it either. Not many

of them did. The surgical ICU was not a place you were sent if you

had a generally good prognosis.

Finally, after about a week, Grandmom's fluid was all shifted

back into place & she was stable enough for surgery. Almost all of

her broken bones were in her feet, so we knew from the beginning

they would require multiple surgeries. She got through the first one

with flying colors, and that night we slept in a hospital room instead

of the waiting room. It felt like a luxury hotel. Early the next

morning, she woke up for the first time since the accident. When she

finally spoke, I felt a thousand elephants get up and walk off of my

shoulders. By my logic, she was awake, she was talking, and she was

going to be fine. I could finally start to relax.

The air is thick and hot and the sand is warm on my feet and little pieces of it are stuck under my fingernails. I'm stretched out on a towel and have successfully wallowed the sand underneath me into a comfy shape, complete with a lump under my head for a pillow. There's a layer of dried salt covering my body and tongue and drying out my sun-bleached hair. I can tell I'm starting to sunburn, but the waves are gently kissing the shore and the breeze is light and together they're lulling me to sleep so I don't really care about my pinking skin. We've been here since 6am because we wanted to watch one more sunrise. Our early arrival was followed by a day of snorkeling and diving for shells and has left me sapped of the energy reapplying sunscreen requires. I am at my peak relaxation and I start to doze, soaking in the sunshine on my skin and the smell of the salt spray. As I slowly drift to sleep, I see myself stand up and walk into the water. I leave my snorkel gear on the shore without a glance and glide into the waves, sinking deeper and deeper until I'm fully submersed in the emerald green world. Somehow, I can breathe beneath the surface, and I swim further and further out, spotting several familiar kinds of fish as I go. I'm entranced by their colorful scales, shades of blue and silver and yellow dancing in the filtered sunlight. My otherwise subpar human legs and feet magically propel me like a rocket through the water. It's exhilarating. Shadows emerge from the edges of my visibility. They click and chirp at me and nudge me with their bottle-shaped noses. They let me scratch their bellies and trill excitedly when I hit spots they can't reach on their own. I laugh and we start to play, racing each other through the water and enjoying the ease with which we move in this world. The babies chirp and play excitedly in the waves, darting around the rest of us like hummingbirds. One of the adults looks at me pointedly with one of his big, grey eyes and we fly to the surface together, breach, then reenter the waves with a graceful splash. We play like this for hours, turning the breaches into flipping contests, chasing bubbles, and tossing sand dollars to one another in an underwater game of fetch. Inevitably, the sun above the surface begins to set and I know my time is up. We say our goodbyes and I slowly swim toward the shore. As I get closer, I can hear the beach calling my name.

"Rebecca…" It's barely audible. I resent it for calling me away from my magical day even though I'm leaving of my own accord, but I keep swimming at a slow, steady pace until I can reach the sandy bottom with my feet again.

"Rebecca, come on…" I hear again. The voice is a little louder this time, but still a gentle beckoning in the background of the sounds of the surf and the sandy shores glistening in the waning sunlight. I sink below the surface and swim in spirals through the water, letting the waves carry me at their will. When it's shallow enough, I do handstands in the surf and dive down to examine shells and hermit crabs. I realize my ability to breathe below the surface is waning. Reluctantly, I turn and start plodding toward the beach.

I'm about 20 yards from the shore when I hear, **"REBECCA. GET UP. IT'S TIME TO GO."**

I jolt awake with a start, reality smacking me in the face like icy water and stiff from napping in the sand. Shit. That was my favorite dream. "Come on. Get your stuff packed up. Let's go home," says my mother. The purring, soft voice of the sand has been replaced by hers, drowsier than normal from a day spent in the sun but tinged with her love for timeliness and organization. I slowly stretch my sleepy muscles, take one more big breath of the ocean air, then get up and start to pack my sandy beach gear. After a few minutes, our crew of 7 has packed up all of our stuff and is trudging through the sugar bowl sand back to the car. We dust off our feet, pile in, and head back to the house where 4 of us will shower and load our luggage. We're leaving Pensacola in the morning and going back to Mississippi, which is where we live and go to school. It's where my friends are and where my horses live in our pasture and where the barn my Dad built with my Papa Jack stands on the land that our house sits on thanks to my Mom's ancestors. Differently from the rest of my family, though, I'll be leaving home instead of returning to it.

Support

At some point I went back to school. I'd spend a few days in Hattiesburg for class, attempting to exist normally and secretly having panic attacks while cuddling with my twenty-five-pound Schnauzer mix, Scruffy, at night when I couldn't stifle my feelings anymore. Then I'd drive to Jackson for a few days to relieve Mom. She and I and Grandad and Aunt Winnie took turns being with Grandmom. We made sure she was never alone, even though it was exhausting for us. Since this incident, I've worked in a hospital and witnessed many other people going through many horrible situations, some eerily similar to ours. A saddeningly large number of our patients went through their last days alone, and I always wondered what things led to that kind of an ending to their stories. Grandmom was my favorite human and our family's matriarch, so we made sure she was never alone, which meant I commuted between Jackson and Hattiesburg a lot. Mom used her FMLA rights to take time off. Grandad and Aunt Winnie made the 3-hour round trip every single day. And people visited. Every single day. Even though we were all impossibly tired and stressed and still in shock, we never wanted for company. "

The days trudged on and at some point, I realized I was mentally tiptoeing around living in reality. I slept, but not well and I never dreamed. I got up every day and showered and brushed my teeth and got dressed and did what I had to do to get through each day, but I didn't engage with life. I didn't go out with friends because I didn't have time. Even if I'd had the time, I had absolutely zero energy beyond what it took to exist. I went to school, I sat with Grandmom, and when I wasn't doing one of those two things, I was subconsciously keeping myself busy enough with schoolwork and binge-watching Grey's Anatomy to not fall apart. I had thought the adrenaline had shut off that day in the SICU waiting room bathroom, but it was still trickling through my system all day, every day, keeping me from mentally and physically collapsing but also preventing me from resting and recharging. So I just survived and didn't think about the rest.

One day, I was in the apartment I shared with my best friend Hannah. We'd been best friends at that point for about fifteen years and existed comfortably together. This day, I was milling about after class and tending to Scruffy while Hannah was talking to me from the sofa. After a few minutes I realized I was struggling to focus on her words. The words in my head were screaming much louder than she was talking. They were saying things like, "What if she dies? What if you're not there? How did this happen? What did I do wrong? What if her heart can't take all the surgeries?" They'd been saying those things since the accident but today they were so much louder than usual. Hannah's words kept being drowned out and I was getting increasingly frustrated. I wanted to be able to hear her but at the same time the voices in my head were so demanding and what they had to say felt so much heavier and more important. I started to get frustrated with her instead of myself. Finally, she said something that pushed me over the edge. I don't remember what it was, but I remember my vision going white and my heart feeling like it would explode from the stress, and I remember yelling something about not being able to help her with her problems. Then I melted into a panicky, tearful tirade about Grandmom. I remember sinking onto the couch next to Hannah and falling over into her arms, and her holding me and letting me cry. Then I finally said the things my brain had been screaming for weeks.

"Hannah, what if she dies?" I sobbed into her.

"I've been waiting for this to happen," she said gently.

Then she quietly held me until I stopped crying and the voices in my head were finally quiet. Crying on the couch with Hannah is the only time during this whole thing I ever let myself break. The next time I switched my emotions back on was February 4th, 2014, some 4 months later.

One night, I got to the hospital just before dark. Mom updated me on Grandmom's condition and the day's events, and I sent her home to rest. I made up my little hospital chair/bed and started to settle in. Then I realized I didn't have my phone charger. Panic ensued. Normally that would be no big deal. Normally I'd just let it die and go charge it in the car the next morning. But this wasn't normally. I was the connection my family had to Grandmom. I was in charge while they got much needed rest. If something happened, I wouldn't be able to call them immediately, and vice versa. At this point, it was very late at night, but I was desperate, so I racked my brains.

I couldn't leave, so going to buy a charger wasn't an option. The hospital gift shop was also closed so that was out. Then I remembered I knew people in town. *Score!* I hoped for the best and texted the only friend I knew I had in Jackson, a friend from high school named Owen. I told him what I needed and where I was and crossed my fingers. Almost immediately he responded, "Be there in ten minutes!" I almost cried I was so relieved. Ten minutes later, I met him in the front lobby and gave him a big hug, then promptly went back to my makeshift couch-bed in Grandmom's room and passed out, the phone charger stress having zapped my small store of extra energy.

Support from my friends got me through Grandmom's time in the hospital. I've been very lucky in this life to have more really good friends than most people, and all of them were there for me when I needed them. My best friends, Hannah, Anna, and Julia, kept up with me and provided distractions when I needed them. We'd all been best friends since middle school and had remained close after moving to college. My other close friends from childhood all checked in regularly too, and they and my friends and sorority sisters from college provided some normalcy in my very abnormal life. I was thankful for them every day.

Moving

Eventually Grandmom was doing well enough to leave UMMC. Her fluid had shifted back nicely, and she'd had a preliminary surgery to fix her feet. She couldn't go home, she couldn't stay in her room at UMMC, but she could go to a step-down facility since she didn't require so much care and needed more physical rehab during the interim between surgeries than actual medical care. We had a choice between the tiny, rural hospital closer to Pleasant Valley and the better hospital in the town where my younger brother, Ben, and I went to school. When I realized everyone was leaning toward the tiny hospital because it was closer to home, I freaked out. I'd seen so many people go into that building and never come out, and I knew how small it was and I knew that meant they didn't have access to as many resources as other hospitals and I knew my Grandmom wasn't going to the death hospital, dammit. So I protested with as much energy as I could muster but it wasn't up to me and off to the tiny hospital we went. In most ways, this turned out to be a good decision. One of my best friends ended up being Grandmom's CNA, and everybody knows everybody in our tiny little town, so when shit hit the fan it wasn't hard to pitch a big enough fit to get it handled. And shit definitely hit the fan.

At this point I'd said goodbye to my life in Hattiesburg, moved back into Mom and Dad's house, and was commuting the 2.5 hours one way to USM two days a week to finish my degree. I had also dropped the education part of my Spanish major so I could graduate on time while going to school part-time that semester. My new priority was to focus on Grandmom and graduating, and I was only doing what I had to do to get the heck out of college. Dad was working, Ben was back at school in Starkville, and Mom was still on FMLA. We were all running on pure adrenaline and determination (and caffeine in my case).

Shortly after getting Grandmom settled into the small-town hospital, we started noticing she was sleeping more than she had been. A lot more. It was enough to worry us, so we started investigating. I spent the first ten years of my professional life working in pharmacies, and in 2013/2014 when this was happening, I'd had enough experience in the field to know the big 'what not to dos' for most medications so I requested a copy of her med list. When I finally got my hands on it I was immediately shocked at how long it was. It's normal for long-term inpatient med lists to be somewhat lengthy, but hers was one of the longest I've ever seen. As I browsed over the unnecessarily long list and saw why it was so long, I felt angry heat spreading through my body. She was on the standard hospital meds for preventing blood clots and treating pain and solving digestive issues, but she was also prescribed multiple benzodiazepines and antipsychotics 'as needed.' I kept reading and saw the benzodiazepines were prescribed to her as sleeping medications. She wasn't having any trouble sleeping. She was, however, having a LOT of trouble staying awake. Which meant somehow, she was getting these 'as needed' medications way more often than they were needed. I was disgusted.

I found out later that day that Mom and Dad had discovered the same thing during their morning shift and had already made several phone calls. By the time we thought we had the issue resolved, they made a lot more phone calls to all kinds of doctors and all of us yelled at a lot of nurses. We did get her med list changed, but I don't think we ever did get the nurses to stop cramming pills down her throat that she didn't need. By the time she left the teeny tiny hospital, I was very thoroughly disillusioned and very, very angry.

While she was still there and we were still fighting to get her meds changed, Grandmom had another surgery on her feet. This time her feet looked like something out of a sci-fi movie, or two very metallic porcupines. She had about 20 rods sticking out of each foot in all directions and tons of plates and pins under the skin to hold her bones together while they slowly healed. During the day she liked to keep a sheet gently draped over them so she didn't have to stare at them all day, but sometimes when people would come visit, she'd have one of us pull the sheet back so she could show off her spikes.

Putting her feet back together took four surgeries over as many months. After surgery 3 we moved to a rehab and nursing center in Brookhaven. It was across the street from the "better" hospital I'd wanted to go to instead of the tiny one, and Grandmom got a roommate. She was in her late 90s and almost totally deaf, but she was calm and sweet and good company. I enjoyed having another person in the room with us, even if we didn't talk much. At this point, Grandad had also hired a lady we knew to sit with Grandmom on days one of us couldn't be there. Mom had to go back to work, which was just up the block from the rehab center, and the rest of us needed a reprieve, so we were all super thankful for her. I was still commuting to school two days a week and the other days, I was with Grandmom.

The rehab center days were the best days. Grandmom was starting to act more like herself, we yelled at her nurses enough they mostly quit cramming pills down her throat so she was able to stay awake and talk to us while we were there, and she was getting fantastic physical therapy. After a few weeks, she started putting weight on her feet again, and one day I walked in and she joyously announced, "I stood up today!" She'd had help, of course, but going from forty steel spikes in her feet to standing upright was enough to put her smile back on her face.

I can still smell the way the hallways smelled at that rehab facility. I can still feel the rough carpet in the waiting area, and I can still hear the buckles on my brown leather boots jingle as I walked toward Grandmom's room. I wore those boots every day during Grandmom's stay at the tiny hospital and the rehab facility. They were the boots Mom had bought me for Spain when I still thought I'd be studying abroad that semester. They were intended to carry me miles and miles around Spain, to new places and adventures and fluency. Instead, they carried me miles and miles down hospital and rehab facility hallways. They paced in circles with me. They held me up when I wanted to collapse under the absolute absurdity of the fact that my Grandmom was probably permanently broken and that my life was being flipped inside out. They dug into my legs when I sat on the floor of the rehab facility's bathroom and took slow, deep breaths to stop the oncoming waves of panic when it was hard to keep it at bay. They carried me outside onto the lawn the first day Grandmom was allowed to go outside since the accident. Then, eventually, they carried me into another ER, held me upright one more time, then walked me out when my legs couldn't.

I'm on the bow of the boat and my feet are dangling down, occasionally dipping into the waves as the boat crests and dips with them. I close my eyes and listen to the wind whipping in my ears. The sun is warm on my skin and I'm the kind of tired that comes from spending the day on the water. As I rest my head on my arms which are propped on the bow rail, the movement of the boat changes from the bouncy wave-chopping movement I'm still so familiar with to a gentle gliding. It feels more like a bird flying through the sky than a boat on water. I open my eyes and gasp. I'm no longer on the boat; I'm sitting cross legged atop a Giant Manta Ray. I can feel her smooth, soft skin and her dark black wings are a sharp contrast to the bright blue water we're flying through. She glides smoothly over the vibrant coral reef below, her wings gently moving up and down. I watch, entranced as the colors glow up at me. Parrotfish, sergeant majors, butterfly fish, nurse sharks, elkhorn coral, brain coral, fire coral, sponges, octopuses, and countless other types of reef flora and fauna make up the rainbow scene. Suddenly, the ray dips down sharply and zips between two huge reef walls. We're surrounded by sharp edges jutting out in our path, but she moves deftly to avoid every obstacle. I laugh with exhilaration, throw my head back, and spread out my arms as we soar through the warm waters. Suddenly, she turns and swims straight up and I tumble off her back. I sink for a few seconds, then my feet turn to fins and I start booking it for the surface. I breach, then smack back down into the water with a loud THUD.

"OOF!!" I shout, waking up from my dream entangled in my sheets and half on the floor of my bedroom. My alarm is blaring, and I sigh heavily. What I wouldn't give to be back on that manta instead of facing another day of school and hospitals.

Snow

One day in late January 2014, Mississippi got hit with a freak snowstorm. In Mississippi, one inch of snow counts as a snowstorm since there's no road salt, nobody has chains or shovels or anything like that. This time, though, we got about six inches which promised to be disastrous. So, when the flakes started falling, the whole state shut down. Mom and Dad and Ben and I were trapped at the house for two days, and nobody else could get out to see Grandmom, so we called her frequently and made the best of it. She was improving every day and generally in good spirits, so we welcomed the reprieve and embraced the weather. We drove from our house to the highway and watched people slowly spin out on the ice and drift into the medians (prime entertainment where we lived), and Ben started a fire in the snow in the middle of the woods with an old earplug and some jean lint. He's a good boy scout, and for a few beautiful minutes free of heart monitor beeping and hospital pages and antiseptic smells, we ate deer sausage warmed up over the fire together and just existed in the beautiful, icy white trees and talked about things that weren't surgery and physical therapy and med lists.

A guaranteed result of snow in Mississippi is car wrecks, so when we could finally get out of the valley, Dad and Ben and I responded to a few. It occurred to me at some point during the day that maybe that should have been stressful considering what our lives were like as the result of a major car accident, but I couldn't quite tap into that feeling so I just kept moving. After we responded together to a couple of cars that had slid into the median, I worked one wreck by myself. Dad and Ben were across the highway and two other first responders were at another one just up the road from us. As I approached the vehicle I was responding to which had spun out and slid into a ditch, I started to assess the scene. The car looked fine which boded well for the people inside. I approached the driver's side and a blonde woman in her forties rolled the window down. I could see she had one passenger; a young girl who looked just like her. They both looked unharmed and immediately assured me they were fine, so I went through the list of questions and confirmed they weren't hurt, then helped them get out of the ditch. I waved them off and was about halfway across the highway when it hit me: everyone was fine. It was the first wreck I'd gone to since Grandmom's and everybody was fine. Nobody was even scratched. I stopped and let a few tears of relief escape, then trotted off to help Dad and Ben at their scene.

About a week later, all the snow was long gone and it was absolutely POURING down rain (Mississippi has great weather). Naturally, we all loaded up to go see Grandmom. Mom and I were in her car ahead of Dad and Ben in Dad's car, and about halfway to town and Mom and I saw a small truck hydroplane off the road into the trees. I felt my adrenaline kick in and sat up straight in my seat, knowing we'd pull over.

"You wanna stop?" Mom asked, already slowing down.

I said, "Yes! Pull over. I'll jump out."

So she did, and I jumped out into the torrential rain and jogged to the wrecked truck. As I got to the tailgate Dad and Ben were walking toward me from the other side. Dad said Mom had already called 911, so she and Ben got in her car and headed to go see Grandmom and Dad and I stayed on scene. Ben wasn't ever as interested in emergencies as we were, so that wasn't a surprise. Unlike the snowstorm accidents, this wreck caused some damage. The driver was a dad and his two little girls were with him. The truck had taken out a swath of young pine trees and the windshield was shattered, so it was clear there was some force behind the impact which meant more potential for injury. The truck was also on a slope, which made it a more difficult situation for responders. Dad clambered to the driver and began his assessment, and I went to check on the little girls.

The one in the front seat had some pretty deep cuts on her arms from the airbag and one on her forehead. She also told me she was dizzy. The girl in the backseat looked unscathed and was alert and oriented. I helped her get out of the car and by then more first responders had arrived with an ambulance. Dad directed them to get the oldest girl out first and put her on a spine board, so as they did that I took the littlest girl to a van that had appeared nearby and sat her inside where it was dry.

I looked around for something to help warm her up and spotted a roll of blue shop towels so I grabbed a few and helped her pat her arms and hair. I thought about going back and helping out at the scene, but there were already too many people there and I knew I'd be in the way, so I stayed put. The girl I was with was obviously worried about her dad and her sister, so I started telling her stories to keep her distracted and calm. I sat her in a volunteer's passenger seat facing away from her family laid on the side of the road and I told her about the beach in Pensacola and my horses and she told me about her favorite TV shows and her mom.

"Oh! Where is Mommy?!" she asked, realizing she needed her.

"She's on her way!" I reassured her. I'd heard a couple of medics saying as much to her Dad on our way to the van.

I changed the subject back to My Little Pony, which she'd just be telling me about. After a little while, her mom got there so I walked her to the ambulance where her sister and Dad were loaded up and ready to go to the hospital. I spoke briefly to her mom and made sure she took over for me, then turned to go find Dad. Before I could step away from the ambulance, a tiny hand wrapped around mine and pulled down HARD. I turned around and saw the little girl was staring up at me, her fingers wrapped around mine in a vice grip. I squatted in front of her and she gently cupped my face in her hands. She took a big breath, looked me in the eyes and, with the depth of a grown woman said, "You are my angel, and we can take it from here."

Immediately, every hair on my body stood at attention and I had to consciously catch my breath. *We can take it from here.* I'd heard almost those exact words before almost five months earlier at a very different accident scene. The person who'd said them to me then had been first on the scene and had placed Grandmom's hand in mine as she said them then vanished into thin air. Nobody had known who I was talking about that day and I hadn't been able to track her down.

I snapped back to the present and smiled as big as I could at the little girl who was still holding my face. I could tell she knew I was emotional, and after a beat she reached down from my face and held my trembling hands as we stared into each other's eyes. I tried not to tear up. After a few shaky breaths I managed to squeak out, "Thank you, sweetheart." I gave her tiny hands a gentle squeeze before I turned and walked away.

I found Dad and jogged to his truck with him, and we went home and changed into dry clothes then went to Brookhaven. It was Super

Bowl day, so we all piled into Grandmom's room and watched the game with her. Before the accident, she'd never watched much football, but while she was in the hospital she watched as much as she could. I think it helped keep her distracted without requiring too much effort. Around halftime, Mom and Dad decided to go home since the weather was still bad and it was getting dark. Ben had class the next day, so he left with them.

I stayed with her after they went home that night so we could finish the game, and she and I had heart to heart chats while the sounds of the game filled the background with noise. We talked about my future and my career path, we talked about my relationships, we talked about my tattoos (she said she liked them), and we both relaxed a little bit. By the time the fourth quarter rolled around I could feel a real smile on my face, the first one I'd smiled in months. On my way out of her room, I kissed Grandmom on the cheek, then grabbed her left hand in my right hand and said, "I love you, see you soon," just as I had on my way out of every other room every other time I left her since the wreck. Those words mean more to me now than I ever thought they would.

That was the day I got my Grandmom back. I wanted to cry in

relief on my way home that night, but I couldn't no matter how hard

I tried. I'd been emotionally shut down for too long to cry on

demand, so I smiled and sang to music the whole way home instead.

The phone rang. I answered. They spoke. I screamed. Then I blinked and I was there. The cars were ripped into large chunks of metal and strewn all over the road. It was sunny and eerily silent. A wheel spun slowly on its axle though separated from its car. I stood perfectly still, knowing I needed to make very sure I made no mistakes here. First: find Grandmom. Second: fix her. Third: don't let go of her hand. I spotted her lying on her side next to the road about 50 yards away, toward the bridge and the wreckage of the other car. I walked to her calmly and deliberately. When I reached her, I knelt down and started talking to her.

"Hey Grandmom. It's me. Don't be scared. I'm going to fix you right up, then we'll go home. Okay?" I cooed, as though sweet talking a horse into letting me put a saddle on it for the first time.

She just stared at me and nodded. I assessed her injuries which were mostly broken bones that I could snap back into place like tinker toys, so I started sorting them into piles of pieces I knew went together. I'd reassembled all but two of them when I heard it: the whirring of the chopper. My adrenaline started pumping again. I knew if I wasn't finished by the time it landed I'd fail and she'd die again. I quickly snapped the last two tinker toy bones together and grabbed her hand.

"Okay you're all fixed up. Now let's go for a ride and let the doctor make sure you're all better then we'll be done."

She silently stared back into my gaze, her fear reflecting my own. The chopper landed. The medics marched over. They slid the spine board under her and lifted her onto the stretcher. I kept repeating my mantra in my head: "Don't let go of her hand." They wheeled her over to the door and I held on. They slid her into the cockpit and laid her on the floor right next to the door, letting her right arm dangle out as I still held on. I knew they'd do it just like they'd done it every time before, so I wasn't surprised when I was left standing on the pavement as the chopper lifted into the air. "Don't let go of her hand. Don't let go of her hand. Don't let go of her hand." I repeated over and over as we slowly left the ground. Soon I was dangling in the air, attached only by our joined hands. The pilot swung us around and started racing to the hospital. I held on tightly. The first few trees were easy to dodge. I'd had lots of practice. After a few minutes I'd made it farther than ever before though, and it started getting more difficult not to let my hand slip out of hers. The trees started appearing out of nowhere and they were getting bigger, so it was harder to not get raked off by one of them. Suddenly all of the trees disappeared. The air was clear. It was just me dangling from Grandmom's arm and the chopper and clear, blue skies. Was this it? Had I finally won? I searched frantically for an obstacle I'd missed but found nothing. I whooped with joy, convinced I'd finally done a good enough job to keep her.

I looked up, caught her eye, and shouted, "We did it! We won!" She smiled back, but sadly, as though she knew something I didn't. I lowered my gaze, *confused by her reaction. Then SMACK!! I felt my body slam into the huge brick wall of the hospital in the same moment that I felt her hand slip from mine. I screamed in anguish as I fell through the air, devastated by how close I'd gotten to keeping her just to lose AGAIN. I wept as the ground rocketed toward my face. As I collided with it, I woke up on the floor of my room, soaked in tears and sweat and still clasping my blanket as though holding a hand in mine.*

Gone

That was February 2, 2014. On February 3, 2014, I had class. I called Grandmom on the way home from Hattiesburg and we chatted briefly. Mom and Dad had been with her all day and gotten her a hot dog and a milkshake and she had eaten all of it, which, considering her scant appetite through this whole ordeal, was major progress. She didn't have much energy on the phone, but her voice sounded strong and her personality was still shining through the exhaustion. We talked for a few more minutes, but it was late and she was tired, so I let her go to sleep. I smiled the whole way home again, and I went to sleep that night still smiling because I could finally, finally glimpse a little bit of light at the end of this dark, heavy tunnel. After four and a half months of an unimaginable nightmare, Grandmom was coming back to us. Maybe, just maybe, we'd come out of this okay.

I opened my eyes, awoken by the sound of waves crashing on a nearby shore. I looked straight ahead into a grey sky and realized I was lying down. I wiggled my toes and fingers and felt sand between them, then I slowly sat up. I was on a beach, our beach, and it was gloomy. The wind was whipping through the sea grasses and the white capped waves were pummeling the sandy shoreline. I looked to my left, then to my right. I was alone. I stood up and walked toward the water. I loved these wild days with the ocean, when she got to show off some of what she could do. As I sank my right foot into the wet sand at the wave line, I sensed someone was near me. I quickly looked to my left and saw Grandmom had appeared. I wasn't surprised because it felt like she'd been there the whole time. She smiled at me, and I smiled at her, then we both stared out at the waves. One, two, three waves crashed onto my toes. I closed my eyes and breathed in the stormy, salty air. As I exhaled, I opened my eyes again and looked toward Grandmom. When our eyes met, I felt a slight shift in the air around us, like the storm was changing gears. Grandmom's previously smiling eyes faltered and became sad. I looked at her quizzically and she gently shook her head once, as if to say, "No, don't ask." At that moment I suddenly knew I'd be leaving the beach soon, so smiled a sad smile and said, "I love you, see you soon." She said, "I love you too babe." Then I looked to the sky, took a deep breath, and closed my eyes.

"Wake up. Grandmom had a heart attack."

It was 4:45 in the morning on February 4th and Mom had shaken

me awake, dropped a bomb in the form of two short sentences, then

vanished. I immediately snapped right back into crisis mode. Mom

and Dad were peeling out of our driveway by the time I stood up, so

Ben and I got dressed and followed. As I got dressed, I had a

stomach-turning sense of déjà vu. This was the second time in less

than 5 months I had thrown on whatever shoes I could find, jumped

in a truck, and consciously turned on my adrenaline. This time was a

little different though. Five months ago, I hadn't known what was

waiting at the end of the drive. This time, deep down in my gut, in

the place where you know things before you know them, I knew

there was no reason for Ben to speed or to turn on his flashers. It was

the same reason Grandmom had been with me on the beach just a

few short minutes ago.

As we stepped across the threshold into the emergency room, the

nurses directed us to a room to the left. Before I even looked toward

the door, I knew the worst had happened. I knew in every synapse

of every neuron that my favorite human, my best friend, the person most like me on this Earth, had left without me. I knew I would walk through that nondescript, greyish door into a room and see a body but no person. I knew all of our hard work and tears and sleepless nights over the last few months had been erased in a single moment. I knew my favorite person in the whole world was still standing on that beach in my dream, watching the waves with slightly sad eyes.

Ben and I crossed the space between the nurses' desk and the door in a millisecond that took a thousand years and he swung open the door. I'd been preparing myself for the whole drive to the hospital, but when I looked into that room and saw Mom and Grandad standing by the bed in the otherwise empty room, and watched Mom slowly shake her head, all I heard was crashing waves and a piercing, guttural scream that made my hairs stand on end. I was wondering who was screaming like that in an emergency room before daylight when someone hugged me, and I realized it was me. I managed to stop the scream I never agreed to allow to start, walked over to not-Grandmom-anymore, leaned down, and kissed her gently on the cheek that would never be warm again.

"I love you. See you soon," I whispered in her unhearing ear, then

I walked out of the empty room.

Across the hall, Mom and Grandad were talking to a doctor. I walked in and the scream I'd cut off started to bellow its way back out. My body started shaking and I felt myself involuntarily going into a meltdown. Mom reached over quickly and squeezed my hand, grounding me.

"Shhhh. Breathe. We have to be strong for Grandad," she muttered. I swallowed hard, shoved everything down again, and somehow got through the next few minutes. The hospital staff talked to Mom and Grandad about what happens next when somebody dies, paperwork was signed, then we all went home without Grandmom, again and for the last time.

Aftermath

I'd lost people before. A few of my friends were in a car accident in high school, older relatives passed away, the usual deaths people deal with in their early years. Grandmom's death was an entirely different monster and it knocked me breathless. For weeks I felt like I couldn't physically move air in and out of my lungs without astronomical effort. Hannah called me sometime on the 4th and I was walking down our driveway trying to figure out how to breathe without wearing myself out. I couldn't cry in front of Grandad, so I cried on the phone with Hannah.

"I don't know how to live in a world where she doesn't exist," I sputtered between panicked sobs.

I still don't.

People came from all over for the visitation and funeral. The visitation was at the funeral home in Brookhaven, and the flowers were perfect. We had several of Grandmom's watercolor paintings on display, and we played Edelweiss in the background. Hundreds of people were there. The people who visited her in the hospitals and people we hadn't seen in years and people I'd never met. It was

amazing to see how many people loved, and still love, Grandmom.

My sorority twin, Mary, came to be with me and Mom's best friend

came to be with her, so we had people immediately nearby to help

us remember to function.

We chose sky blue for the casket color because it matched the van

that we knew had saved Grandmom for us, even if it was just for a

few more months. We released lilac and sky-blue balloons at the

wreck site as the hearse drove her body by en route to the funeral at

the family church down the road from our houses. There was good,

Scott family singing during the funeral and I wrote a eulogy of sorts

for the preacher to read. It made everyone cry except for me. I was

all out of tears by then and settled comfortably into my grief-ridden

numbness. It was a beautiful, sunny, warm day. Hannah was

working at Disney World that semester so she couldn't come, but her

dad, who I've always called my other dad, showed up and surprised

us, which was wonderful because I needed any piece of Hannah I

could get that day. Family and friends were all around us. We

laughed and they cried and we ate, and Grandmom would have

loved it. We buried her in the family cemetery behind the family church, and she would love that too. It was the perfect send off for my favorite person.

The funeral was on February 8th, and everyone left on February 9th, so February 10th was the beginning of our new normal. Our lives had totally revolved around Fixing Grandmom for 5 months and figuring out how to fill our days when we no longer needed to take care of her felt impossible. I couldn't read books because my mind wanders when I read, and it would wander to sad things and I'd end up crying every few sentences. I couldn't watch certain movies or TV shows because they'd make me have big scary feelings, so mostly I watched Grey's Anatomy on repeat because it was familiar and somehow managed to muddle through my schoolwork.

Two weeks to the day after Grandmom died, one of my best friends lost her mom. I immediately packed a bag and drove to Hattiesburg, not stopping to consider the fact that I was driving toward a scenario I'd only just come out of myself. I spent the next few nights in Hattiesburg with my friend and our other friends and her family and it was weirdly comforting to be in the funeral scene again, especially when it wasn't for my people. It was like it was a situation I knew how to navigate so I could relax a little bit. Not being an object of everyone's sympathy for a little while was incredibly therapeutic.

I went home after the funeral, and for the next few days I hyper focused on school and deciding what I was going to do with my life since now all of my options were suddenly wide open. I had a fiancée at the time who was planning to go to school in Louisiana the following Fall and I hate Louisiana (for myself, I'm sure it's lovely for other people). I don't even care for New Orleans, which is a cardinal sin where I'm from. I spent a few days apartment hunting in Louisiana, then one night I had a tangible dream that I was on the beach with Grandmom. It felt familiar, but in this dream she looked at me before I woke up and said, "You know where you need to be. Go home." So, the next morning I woke up and decided I wasn't going to Louisiana. I called my then fiancée and told him we could postpone the wedding until I was settled, I talked to my family, and I made the best decision I've ever made. Grandmom was right; I knew where my heart needed to go. So, on May 17th I loaded all of my stuff up in my Subaru Forester, loaded Scruffy into the front seat, and we moved to Pensacola.

Restart

It was a sunny day in mid-May of 2014. I'd woken up that morning as a Pensacola resident for the first time ever and decided the only real way to celebrate was by going to the beach. I hopped out of bed, grabbed one of Grandmom's beach bags from the rack in the garage, threw in a towel, a drink, and a book, and headed out. I found a quiet spot on the sound side at Opal beach and had a peaceful and perfect day. The sun was shining, there was a light breeze, and the water was warm and calm. I stayed for hours, alternating between dozing in the sunshine, reading my book, cooling off in the water, and walking up and down the sand. Somehow, I spent the whole day there and saw no other humans, which is a rare occasion on pretty summer days in Pensacola.

As I was basking in the warm sun, I allowed my mind to wander as much as I safely could. I didn't want to focus on how sad I was over Grandmom or think about how complicated my relationship was with my fiancée. I just wanted to enjoy the beach and focus on happy things. You can only fight your thoughts so much though, so when I let mine wander, it was filled with thoughts I couldn't quite focus on yet because they were too overwhelming. To try to keep things from overflowing too much, I let myself feel sad for a few minutes when the thoughts popped up, then immediately shut them down when they threatened to spill over. It was a practice I was getting pretty good at those days. I was afraid that if I let the big feelings hang around too much they'd take over and I wouldn't be able to stop them or get them under control again. So instead, I gave them a brief moment to breathe, then I turned on my beach music and focused on what was tangible and comfortable. The warmth on my skin, the grains of sand under my fingernails, the water lapping against my shoulders as I sank under the surface, the sounds of seabirds flying overhead. All of these were the perfect combination of soothing and distracting. And so my beach days routine began to take shape: lie in the sun until the scary thoughts take over, swim/snorkel for a bit to distract myself, lie in the sun some more, snorkel, repeat, repeat, repeat. All with a specifically curated beach playlist playing in the background. Distract, distract, distract, or we might lose control of ourselves…

The next day was my first day at my new job. I'd accepted an offer at a local compounding pharmacy before I left Mississippi and I was super excited for it. I'd worked in pharmacies since high school for extra fun money, but this time I was genuinely interested in learning about the company and the industry. I got up the morning of my first day, pulled on my grey scrubs, and headed out. The next eight hours were overwhelming but exciting. Everybody seemed super nice and I could already tell the company was very focused on ethics, a very touchy area in compounding pharmacies. During my lunch break, I was the only person in the breakroom and it was the first quiet moment I'd had all day. As I was munching on my ham sandwich I'd packed, I started thinking about how I'd call Grandmom on the way home and tell her all about it, then I remembered I couldn't do that. Immediately I started to cry involuntarily into my lunch. I quickly snatched a paper towel off the wall to try to quell the flow of tears and snot and started trying to swallow the emotions and gather myself. Crying on my first day?! Unacceptable. I was scrambling for a guaranteed pain-free subject to think about when the break room door swung open and a tall, dark-haired girl I knew was named Jamie walked in.

"Hey! How's it going?" she asked me.

"Pretty good. I'm starting to settle in, I think."

"That's good! My friend Toriee and I are going downtown for

drinks this weekend if you want to come." Friends?! Already! Yes!

I smiled and said, "Sure, that sounds great!"

At that moment, the breakroom door was flung open again and a tangle of limbs and sandy brown hair and freckles awkwardly stumbled into the room, somehow staying upright. The tangle of limbs righted itself and looked up at us. She saw that Jamie and I were staring at her and stuttered, "Oh! Hi! I'm Toriee!......b-bye!" and practically ran out of the room. Jamie and I cracked up laughing.

"So that's Toriee and yes she's always like that," Jamie chuckled.

"Oh good! Me too," I laughed. I decided I liked them both.

For the next few months, we hung out a good bit. We went out downtown together, did dinner dates together, did a couple of beach days together, and went to some concerts. Toriee and Jamie were exactly what I needed at that point. They were fun and free and supportive of each other, and they took me under their wing. They loved having fun and they were always doing something, which suited my need to never spend too much time with my thoughts just fine. After a couple of months, I started to feel like myself again. Most of the time anyway.

I got to know my other coworkers too, and really started to feel at home in a place I'd always loved more than where I was from. My job was interesting, I was learning a lot, making new friends, and settling in comfortably to my new life. I'd even managed to smooth things over with the fiancée and we were doing better. Not great, but better. Things were looking up, and I was as happy as I could be considering everything I'd gone through. My first month in my new home went swimmingly, and I was thrilled.

I walk into the Firestone house and the smell of her hits me in the face like a brick wall. It takes my breath away and I stop in my tracks. I slowly, carefully inhale and have no choice but to let the emotions wash over me. I close my eyes as the tears I did not plan to acknowledge start to fall and I steady myself, taking several slow, deep breaths. When I open my eyes, I'm surrounded by a waist-deep pile of pale-yellow crocs that stretches as far as I can see. They're heavy against my skin, and the pressure of them on my legs is making my heart rate skyrocket and suddenly it's hard to breathe. I try to take a step, but more crocs erupt from the new ones I've touched, just like that bank vault in the Harry Potter movies. I freeze, throwing my eyes desperately from side to side, searching for an exit. Nothing. There is only me and the crocs and four white walls with no doors. I feel the panic start to rise. Tears are streaming down my face and I can't catch my breath. I muster the air I have left and let out a blood-curdling scream that sounds familiar.

Liberation

I jerk awake, the scream still echoing in my ears, and shake my head a little to clear the nightmare from it. It's mid-June and Mom, Dad, Ben, and the fiancée all come down for the weekend. The fiancée and I had been fighting a lot about his general refusal/inability to get his life together and it was becoming clear that our lives were taking starkly different paths. The idea of having to fake happiness all weekend was daunting, but I promised myself I'd just make it through this visit and see how I felt after that. Adding to my sour mood that day was the fact that it was also the weekend of the zombie run and all of my new friends were going. Toriee and Jamie would be there, and so would my new friends Josh, Setara, and Cat. This would be my first social event with everyone and I'd been excited to join them before the fiancée had decided to come visit with the fam. I knew I should have been excited to see him, but I'd really enjoyed the last month on my own and instead of being excited I was disappointed and anxious.

The whole day of their arrival I had knots in my stomach. They got in on a Friday, and everything went smoothly that evening. We had dinner, hung out, then all went to bed so we could be up early the next day to go out in the boat. I relaxed a little at the thought of

spending the day on the boat. Maybe spending time together in my

happy place would be a good thing for the fiancée and me. I hoped

he'd see how happy I was in Pensacola and realize he needed to

grow up and do what it took to be there with me, or at least establish

a career path of some sort.

Throughout the weekend, however, it became apparent he had

zero intentions of doing any of that. I realized almost immediately

that he was still perfectly content with his life the way it was, and

that he still expected me to eventually move back to Mississippi,

which I would not be doing. We had a long chat in my car the night

before he left, and I told him he had a month to get his shit together

or I was walking away. He promised he would, but I didn't believe

him, and the next morning I was relieved when he left. For the next

few weeks, I tried to convince myself it was okay to stay with him.

We'd been together for most of my college career, and he was there

for me during the Grandmom trauma, so it was hard to let go. I

didn't want to volunteer for more heartbreak than I already had.

Then one day I woke up really mad about the whole thing. None of the things we were fighting about were new problems, and he'd

known when he proposed what I valued in a partner. After

everything I had just been through, I was not about to sign up for

anything less than a life that brought me joy. I was at my desk at

work when all of that really hit me, of course. I managed to hold

myself together until my lunch break rolled around. Then I drove

home and called Mom. She let me yell and cry and curse for about 20

minutes, then encouraged me to do what I knew was best, not what I

wanted to be best. I knew she was right, and a week later when I had

the weekend off, I packed a bag and headed back to Mississippi for

the first time since I'd left.

The main plan was to spend the weekend at Mom and Dad's

house and visit everyone back home. I needed to make a pit stop in

Hattiesburg first though, to end things with the fiancée. I'd dug

through the boxes in my room in Pensacola and found the box for

my engagement ring and gathered a few other items of his I wanted

to return. I had my speech planned, and I had arranged to spend that

night with a friend in Hattiesburg so I wouldn't have to worry about

driving for two hours afterward. Before I left Pensacola, I texted the

fiancée to let him know I'd be stopping by that evening. He was excited and I felt terrible letting him believe it would be a good visit, but I knew he at least deserved for this to happen face to face. When I arrived in Hattiesburg I went straight to his apartment, and as soon as he opened the door and I saw his face, I knew I'd made the right decision. He'd deep cleaned his entire apartment, dressed up for the occasion, and he immediately told me he'd enrolled in a program at a community college that would get him started in a stable career. But none of that changed my mind. It was everything I'd been asking him to do. He'd finally done all of it, but it was too little too late. He took one look at my face after filling me in on everything he'd done to try to save us and knew the same thing. I gave him back the ring and his things, we hugged goodbye, then I drove to my friend's house across town. I wasn't sad. I didn't even cry. I just felt relieved to be done with the whole thing. Finally, I could really focus on grieving Grandmom and moving forward; chasing things that made me happy like playing in the ocean, getting to know myself, and after years of craving adventure – *traveling.*

Kayaking

In 2016, I was working as an instructor at the local technical college in the pharmacy tech program. I'd also discovered the wonders of kayaking. I was raised a boat girl and will always be a boat girl at heart. Kayaks have their own advantages, though. For one, you don't need a license to use them. Also, they fit on TOP of your vehicle instead of having to be towed. I happen to have one that's light enough I can carry it myself, and that's a huge perk. They also sit inches above the water and can be silent modes of transportation through water, which opens up so many opportunities to see really cool stuff.

One day in the early summer of 2016, I loaded up the kayak and Scruffy and we headed out. I didn't have a specific plan for the day, I just intended to drive by my usual launch spots and see what looked best. I'd passed up the busy boat ramps in town and was headed out to the island when my boss texted me and said they were headed out to Sand Island if I wanted to join them. That's when the idea hit me. I quickly texted back, "Meet you there in an hour or so!" and headed toward Fort Pickens, ignoring all the "don't do it" screams from Mom's voice in my head as I drove.

There's a pass in Pensacola that cuts between Fort Pickens, which is on Santa Rosa Island, and Fort McRee, which is technically part of the Alabama section of what used to be one long island. Dredging the pass over the decades has resulted in a man-made island right next to Fort McRee which locals have dubbed Sand Island. To get to Sand Island from Fort Pickens, I had to kayak across the pass. This probably doesn't sound like much to those of you who may be less familiar with saltwater lifestyles, but those of you who are might currently be yelling at this book about how I shouldn't do what I definitely did. You guys would probably say, "Hey dummy. Don't kayak across a pass. That's hella dangerous and you might die." Spoiler alert: I did it anyway.

I got to Fort Pickens, got the kayak out to the beach, unloaded Scruffy who I'd brought along since he'd fully embraced beach dog life, and stopped to do my gear check before I hit the water. This is when Mom's voice in my head started screaming at me about those people who got run over by boats, drowned, or got sucked out to sea when they swam across the pass when I was a kid. She was promptly drowned out by me saying, "Yeah but I'm in a kayak! Plus, it doesn't look that far. The water is super calm and there's practically no traffic!" Let's all laugh at past me together.

Anyway, I finished up the gear check, got Scruffy's lifejacket on him, and we loaded up and headed West toward Sand Island. For about the first 30 minutes, it was easy peasy. I was paddling with little to no effort and maintaining course and I was making good progress. Then I suppose I got out past the off-cast of the end of the island and suddenly I was working RIDICULOUSLY hard to move forward instead of sideways. I was huffing and puffing, unable to take a break without getting zipped due South, while Scruffy was snoozing away between my feet. After about 30 minutes of sweat popping work, I finally looked up to see where I was and HOLY CRAP, I was only HALFWAY?! At this point I stopped paddling, thankful to be in a spot I could take a breather, and splashed myself down with nice, cool, pass water. I turned around and looked back at Fort Pickens and seriously wondered if I should turn around, then I looked back at Sand Island and decided I'd come this far and I was no quitter, so I had no choice - I had to persevere!

I mentally reverted to my horse girl instincts - I ducked my head, gritted my teeth, and settled in for the long haul. I started paddling to a rhythm and breathing in time with my strokes and for what felt like days (but was probably only about an hour) that's all that existed. Breathe, pull, breathe, pull, breathe, pull. Finally, I glimpsed the water's color changing under my arm as I reached forward to pull, so I looked up. I'd made it! I poured all the rest of my energy into building up enough speed to beach the kayak on the island and made a mental note to say extra prayers of thanks that night. Scruff and I unloaded and found my boss and settled in for a fun day. Then the storm blew up.

We'd been hanging out for about 45 minutes and the gulf coast did what it does best: changes in an instant. What was initially a beautifully cloudless day instantly turned into a dark, wild thunderstorm. And I was on an island with naught but a kayak for transportation! Thankfully, my boss and her family had a boat with a cabin, so Scruffy and I piled in with them to ride out the storm. Like they usually do, the storm passed in about 30 minutes, and we all hopped back in the water for more sunny fun.

When the time came to go home, I started gathering my gear and prepping for my journey back across the pass. The current had picked up a little after the storm, and traffic was heavier since it was later in the day, but I decided I'd start out way closer inland so if I drifted with the current it wouldn't be too detrimental. I was plotting my course when my boss offered to give me a ride back over. I said, "Oh thanks, but we'll be okay! We're going to stick to the inland route and go fast so we'll be across soon enough." She made me promise to text her as soon as we made it to sand, and I swore I would, then we parted ways.

I got Scruffy loaded up, got all my gear gathered, and started my gear check. As I looked over my oar, I noticed a teeny tiny crack beginning at the joint. "Oh well," I thought, "it should last through this fine, but then I'll have to replace it." I shoved off and started up my breathe, pull rhythm again. I got about 50 breathe pulls in when I felt the oar split and pinch my hand as I tugged it through the water. Immediately, I knew I was in trouble. I felt visions of those people Mom had been yelling at me about in my head that morning bubbling to the surface and quickly shoved them away. I needed to focus! I adjusted my hand position and kept breathe-pulling.

About 20 breathe-pulls later, I looked up and realized I was being pulled out toward the Gulf WAY faster than I had anticipated. Half of my brain tried to stop and plan a solution, but the other half thankfully remembered I was floating on the water that was sucking me out to sea and I had to keep moving, so I breathe-pulled even faster and angled myself away from imminent doom (the open water). At this point I was about a quarter of the way across the pass, and that's when the boats started POURING in from the gulf. I spent the next hour of my life convinced I was going to catch a wake at just the wrong angle and Scruffy and I were going to drown. I was seriously scared I wouldn't make it out of this dumb decision. Mom's voice in my head was eerily silent and every time a boat would go by, I'd steel myself and gear up my legs to shift the kayak with every wave and sub wave that came my way. I was literally smashing my thighs against the inner ledge of the kayak and using that and my exhausted abs/core to lift and turn and balance the kayak. The oar never once entered the water. It would have thrown off the whole thing and we would have flipped. Talk about intense.

After a few wakes, it started to feel like a terrifying dance. Imagine sitting on a big skateboard and going through an obstacle course. That's kind of what this was, and as scary as it was, I know it also pushed me lightyears ahead in my kayaking abilities. Silver lining?

Anyway, there must have been about twenty boats that flew around us in the center section of the pass that day. Once I passed the second channel buoy about seven hundred years later, I knew we'd be okay. We were about halfway down the beach toward the Gulf, way further out than we'd started, and I'd been breathe-pulling for another hour by the time we hit sand. I shoved the kayak as far on the beach as I could with our momentum and then I rolled out of it onto the beach, gasping for air and deeply thankful to be alive. Scruffy jumped out and proceeded to shake over and over, like he was trying to shake off the last 3 hours of our life. I can't say that I blame him. After I caught my breath, I grabbed my phone out of the dry box and texted my boss. Then Scruff and I walked the kayak back around the point, loaded up, and went home to a much-deserved bath and glass of wine (for me). That was a day in which the ocean checked my ego BIG TIME and reminded me that no matter how at home I feel in it, I'm still very, very small and it can easily kill me if it wants to.

I did also have a lot of really cool, not deadly kayaking trips. Shortly after I got the kayak, I decided I was making Scruffy a kayak dog whether he liked it or not. I had just gotten comfortable with the quirks of the kayak and felt like I could get through some Scruffy panic without capsizing, so it felt like a good time to introduce him to water dog activities. That weekend, I loaded up the gear, he hopped in the car, and we headed to Bayou Texar. I got the kayak in the water, loaded up my backpack of supplies, and figured out how to best position Scruffy so I could still do what I needed to do without him being crammed under my knees or something. He ended up getting right between my feet, and for the first half hour he would NOT sit down. He kept trying to climb into my lap and every time the kayak would wobble, he'd whine, so he did a lot of whining. I finally wiggled him back down to my feet and made him lay down, then I let us drift for a while. After about ten minutes, he realized he wasn't going to drown and peeked his head up over my leg to look around. I slowly started paddling and eventually he sat up and relaxed. We paddled around the boat launch area of the bayou for about three hours, then I decided to head out to new water.

We passed under the Bayou Texar bridge and I paddled us over to the marshy grasses that butt up next to the bank where the railroad track is. About two paddles into the grass, Scruffy spotted a tennis ball about 20 feet to my left and LEAPT out of the kayak to go retrieve it before I realized what was happening. I yelled, "What the fuck SCRUFFY?! and grabbed the sides of the kayak as I steadied it. Thankfully, the water was only a couple of feet deep and I had my oar down, so I was able to keep myself from flipping over. When I looked up, Scruffy had gotten the ball and was swimming back to the kayak FAST. I reached over the side as he approached and pushed up on his butt. He plopped his front feet over the keel, pushed off my hand, and hopped right in like he'd been doing it his whole life! Then of course he wanted to play fetch from the kayak, so I positioned myself up in some grasses in shallow enough water I wasn't worried about flipping and started throwing the ball for him. He was having the time of this life, so I decided to go a little deeper. Eventually, I was kayaking, and he was playing swim fetch alongside me all over the bayou. When he got tired, he'd come give me a look like "hey lady, help me get in the boat," and I'd give him a boost and he'd rest for a few minutes, then he'd be right back at it. We played swim fetch for about an hour before I got tired of hurling a soggy tennis ball across the bayou, so I loaded him up and we got ready to head in.

That's when I heard it: the long, slow whistle of an approaching train. Scruffy had never seen a train and I had no idea how he'd react, so I opted to let him experience this new thing from the solid ground instead of the water. I beached us right next to the tracks, quickly got his leash on him, and jogged down the tracks a little way so we wouldn't be so close. About that time, it rounded the bend and the conductor leaned on the whistle. Scruffy immediately lost it. He started scream-growl-barking and running at the train like he was going to eat it up. I scooped him up and talked sweet to him for a bit, trying to ground him. After a few minutes he realized the train wasn't going to eat him and he started to tremble. I remembered how I'd desensitize the horses to scary things like grocery bags and tree branches and socks on the ground. I put Scruffy down and started calmly walking him alongside the train. As we walked with the train he slowly settled down. He kept whining like he always does when he's nervous about something, but at least he'd quit trying to eat it. Within a minute the train was gone and Scruffy was thoroughly traumatized but we'd survived the encounter.

After the train incident we played a little more swim fetch on the way back to the boat launch to help him relax, then we loaded up and headed home for baths and naps. Ever since that day, Scruffy has been a fantastic kayak buddy. He never wobbles, never whines, and never hesitates to load up and come with me. Sometimes he'll even pull the kayak through the water if he jumps in for a swim, which is crazy considering he's a 25lb Schnauzer mix and the kayak alone weighs about 50lbs. In return, I always make sure there's a ball in my backpack so we can play swim fetch when he gets hot.

Bubbles

Since I was little, I've dreamt of living in the ocean. Not just next to it in a pretty beach house with big windows and beach access, actually *in* the ocean. One of the first dreams I ever remember having was of me becoming a dolphin and getting to play with Flipper. The open sea has always been a beautiful, fascinating thing to me, and I've always jumped at any chance to know and see more of it. So, in the Summer of 2015 when Dad said, "Hey, let's get SCUBA certified!" I didn't hesitate to jump in feet first, literally. Ben had gotten his certification the summer before from a local shop and wasn't too pleased with how they taught the essentials, so Dad and I opted for a different shop in town with a better reputation and set up. Eager to get our feet wet, we registered for one of the open water certification (basic) classes and headed to the shop to pick out our gear.

Uncle Ronny came with us, and I think he may have been more excited about the whole thing than we were. The poor guy had been diving alone or with a buddy or two he had in San Destin for decades. He'd even let me play with his gear once or twice to see how I liked it and I know he was hoping one of us would become his new dive buddy. Dad and I picked out a mask, a snorkel, fins, and a dive bag for ourselves. It wasn't required since the shop had rental gear, but we knew we'd use it anyway and wanted our own. Uncle Ronny was a buzzing ball of energy, hopping between Dad and I constantly, answering our questions and offering advice about what gear would be best and why. When we'd made our selections and moved to the cash register with our loot, he insisted upon paying for my snorkel gear. He said he'd been waiting to gear one of us up for a long time, and my birthday was just around the corner, so he wanted to treat me to my first set of gear. His ear-to-ear grin told me everything I needed to know, and I didn't protest.

The next thing I knew, we were four days into training, done with the academic book work, and heading out to jump in the pool. I couldn't WAIT to sink to the bottom, lie on my back, and watch my bubbles float to the surface. Or to float mid-water, suspended and stable, and hang there weightless. Or spin around in circles or do underwater somersaults. I was excited for all of it. We wrapped up the basics and headed outside to the pool behind the dive shop where Slim, our instructor, started showing us how to put on all of our gear. There's a plethora of dive gear out there, and what you need varies based on where you are and what kind of dive you're doing. For our warm pool dive, all we needed was a swimsuit, snorkel gear, a buoyancy controller (BC vest), a regulator, and an air tank. The BC vest is connected to your air tank via your regulator. One arm of the octopus-like regulator connects to the BC and you can inflate or deflate it to control how much you float in the water. Another arm of the regulator has a mouthpiece on it for you to breathe out of, and yet another, shorter arm has a mouthpiece on it so you can let someone else breathe out of it if something goes wrong. I slipped my BC over my air tank and strapped them together, then connected my regulator to them both. Then I inflated my BC so I wouldn't drop to the bottom of the pool like a boulder, popped my mask over my head, slipped my fins on, and *finally* stepped into the pool.

I'd spent my life underwater. Mom and Dad started taking me to the beach and dipping my feet in the waves before I could walk. I started swimming lessons almost before I could read. Everyone always called me a fish, and I had always felt like one. Swimming and being underwater has always been second nature to me. But dropping into that pool in my scuba gear for the first time, knowing I didn't have to worry about surfacing for a breath anytime soon, was a whole new feeling. I dumped some air out of my BC so I wouldn't float to the top like a life raft and immediately headed for the deepest spot of the pool to swim around and get a feel for my gear. As soon as I got to the deep spot, I dropped to the bottom, rolled over, and looked up. It was so. freaking. cool. I blew out a big breath and watched my bubbles float to the surface, then giggled at how much fun it was. After a few minutes of bubbles, I surfaced again and Slim called us all to the shallow end to learn some in-water basics, but I was already dreaming of the open water.

We finished our pool dives that week and our class planned our open water checkout dives for that weekend. We had two separate dives we had to complete before our certification was complete, and we decided to do them in two very different dive locations. Our first one was at Fort Pickens, which is the shoreline that creates one half of the Pass. In other words, the currents can be tricky and dangerous, and the visibility, or distance you can see underwater, isn't always decent. The walk to the water is short though, and the weather was fantastic, so it was a great place to practice our new skills under a little more pressure. For our second dive, we went to a calmer spot down the island called Park East Snorkel Reef. For this one, we had to swim out to a cluster of 'christmas trees' which were just tall, circular, concrete structures with shelves on them that the city had dropped in the water several years prior. The swim out from the beach is a little long, but it's easy if the current isn't too bad.

We got to Park East and suited up, then all waddled into the water in our fins like malformed penguins. We swam out to the reef and did our checkout with Slim, which consisted of skills practice like taking off and replacing our mask underwater, taking our gear all the way off and putting it back on, passing our secondary air source to our buddy, and figuring out our buoyancy. Then we were free to play until our air ran out, and play we did. Dad and I had opted to buddy up with strangers since that would provide more challenge, and my buddy and I had a blast watching the little Blenny fish pop in and out of their holes, swimming with the balls of bait fish that came by and doing flips in the open areas. All too soon, our air tanks were reading low, and it was time to get out of the water, all exiting as newly certified divers. I'd never been more excited to get an ID card in my life.

After getting our open water certifications, I became obsessed with diving and getting new certs. Our dive shop offers a solid variety of courses, and over the next few years I got as many as I could cram into my busy work schedule. First, Dad and I both added NITROX cert to our open waters, which means we can get a different kind of air in our tank that allows us to stay underwater longer. Then, I got my advanced cert which permits me to dive twice as deep as an open water. Finally, I got my rescue diver cert. I figured if the whole family was going to be diving, somebody needed to be qualified to save us if we got into trouble. After rescue, the certifications get much more in depth (pun intended), so I stopped collecting certifications there since I was busy with life at that point, but I didn't stop collecting dives.

Ronny's house was only about an hour and a half East of Pensacola in San Destin, and shortly after I finished my first certification, we started meeting up a couple of times a month or so to dive together. Usually, I'd go to him since he had a boat, but occasionally he came to Pensacola and we did shore dives. When Mom and Dad came to town, and sometimes Ben, we'd all load up and take the boat out to a sunken ship or a reef and go diving together. It became our new favorite hobby as a family, and before we knew it we were planning a trip to the Florida Keys the next summer to see some new dive sites. I had always wanted to visit the

Keys and I'd watched a ton of YouTube videos of people diving there. The water was so blue it looked like CGI and the reefs were absolutely packed with colors and fish. I was so excited I could barely stand it, and every night for months I dreamed about flying underwater with all kinds of sea critters. After the worst two years of my life, I had something huge and happy to look forward to.

Islamorada

On a Wednesday in June of 2015, I left work early, hopped on a plane to Miami, navigated through the Miami airport using the Spanish I remembered from college, then barely made it to my shuttle to Islamorada. This was the first trip I'd been on since Grandmom died, and I was so ready for some relaxation. Mom and Dad and Ben and Uncle Ronny had all arrived at the canal-front vacation house a week before I did since I had to work and had been sending me pictures every day, so I was thrilled to finally be there. It was dark when I got to the house Mom and Dad had rented for the month, but just stepping out of the shuttle into the hot, humid air and smelling the water and hearing the sounds of the creatures that inhabit the mangroves flooded my whole body with a sense of belonging. I walked through the front gate, stopped, and breathed in as deeply as I could. Then I hopped up the steps into the house and walked into our three-story vacation house. Everyone was still awake, so I told them about my adventurous time in the airport and on the shuttle, then headed to bed. My bedroom had windows facing the canal, and I could see the moon behind the palm trees in the yard. I settled in under the covers, facing the window, and fell asleep watching the palm fronds sway in the breeze.

I'm lying on my back floating on the crystal-clear water. My eyes are closed and I'm basking in the sunshine, occasionally dozing off for a few seconds at a time. My ears are under the surface, so I can hear the sounds of the reef below; the gentle whooshing of the sea fans bending back and forth in the waves, the clicking of various critters chomping on the algae or coral or other fish, the occasional chirp of a dolphin passing through in search of a snack. As I listen, my face starts to get too warm, so I take a deep breath, flip over, and dive down to the sea floor. The colors of the reef are almost overwhelming and it's buzzing with life. I stand in the sand next to a wall of coral that's three times taller than me and extends out of my line of sight to my right and left. I gently hop and get high enough to see over the top of the reef wall and discover the expanse stretches as far that direction too. I'm in awe of this massive, healthy ecosystem and start swimming down the wall, observing the interactions of the different species who seem indifferent to my presence. Rainbow blennies pop their heads out of holes in the coral to watch me with their disproportionately large eyes before popping back in when they realize I'm not threatening. Colorful crabs scurry up and down the walls snapping at clumps of algae and other things not visible to my eyes. Sharks glide by in the shadowy water behind me, occasionally parking themselves above the reef for a cleaning from the cleaner wrasse. Rays fly across the top of the wall, their wings beating in time with my excited heart. I squat then leap and twist myself into a slow-motion backflip, then corkscrew through the water away from the reef. I do several flips, then exhale all my air that I somehow hadn't needed. I sink to the bottom, gazing at the backlit surface and saturated with happiness. As I settle onto the sand, I open my eyes and grin at my bedroom window through which I can see the rocky yard, the dark canal water, the mangroves, and the bright blue and green gulf beyond.

The next morning, I woke up still facing the windows in my room to the smell of bacon and coffee seeping in from the kitchen. I could hear that everyone else was up, but I knew they wouldn't be in a hurry, so I basked in the vacation glow for a few minutes. The sun was bright and warm, and I felt more rested than I had in a long time. I took my time getting ready, savoring the hot shower and taking the time to force myself to be present in the day. I didn't want any of this trip to feel like a blur later. I eagerly donned my quick dry shorts, vented boat shirt, and Chacos, a uniform much more suited to my preferred activities than my work scrubs still crumpled on the floor from the night before. Then I walked into the living area to join the others. They were chatting excitedly about the day's plans: diving at Hens & Chicks reef which was a short boat ride from the house. I scarfed down my breakfast, everyone gathered their gear, and we headed out for a watery adventure.

After we got to the dive site, I got geared up in record time and immediately dropped into the water. When my bubbles cleared and I got to see the reef I cried tears of joy. I was blown away. It was so bright and full of fish and all kinds of coral it was overwhelming to look at. The water was a beautiful bright blue, and I could see farther than I'd ever seen underwater. It was like I'd fallen into one of my dreams. That whole first dive I kept shaking my head to make sure it was real, and when we all climbed out into the boat after our tanks ran low, I knew I was hopelessly hooked on the Keys. We spent the next two weeks eating good food, exploring the islands, dodging chickens in Key West, going to museums, swimming with the manatee who loved to visit us in the canal behind the house, searching for a beach, and diving on the most beautiful reefs I'd ever seen outside of my dreams. The visibility stretched as far as we could see, there was abundant reef and transient life, perfect water conditions, and encounters with spotted eagle rays, sea turtles, and sharks that took my breath away.

On the third dive day, we were at Molasses Reef off of Key Largo. We'd been down for about half an hour when I topped a reef wall and saw a pair of giant midnight parrotfish munching on coral together. They were the biggest parrot fish I'd ever seen, probably two feet long each, and both a bright but deep, deep blue color. I was mesmerized. I'd been watching them for what felt like an eternity when the biggest one suddenly turned, looked me in the eye, and swam directly toward me. I froze, not wanting to ruin the moment, then almost reflexively extended my hand toward him. He never slowed, and as he passed, he intentionally brushed his back across my fingertips and shimmied away. I cried happy tears into my mask. It was pure magic.

Later, when Dad and Ben and Uncle Ronny beckoned me over to the ledge they'd been staring under for a while and I stuck my face underneath only to be met by a Moray Eel's mouth FULL of teeth, I screamed in terror. Eels are the only underwater critters I have a healthy level of fear for because of their double set of jaws and razor-sharp teeth (probably also because of the Little Mermaid movie). I back paddled away from the eel as quickly as I could and swam up to the top of the reef wall they were diving on and I was greeted by a school of silvery jackfish darting in and out of purple sea fans. I stretched out my arms so they gently brushed the tops of the fans as I swam over and joined the school of jackfish for a trip down the reef wall. It was much cooler than the eel, and when I closed my eyes, it felt like I was flying.

By about the third dive of the trip, I was fed up with my hair. It was longer than I liked it and wouldn't stop getting tangled around my regulator/air tank neck to the point where I couldn't move my head when I got out of the water. The ends were already getting dried out from the salt water, and I had a desperate urge to chop it all off. When we got home that afternoon I googled hair salons nearby and the next morning I drove to a salon next to a Winn Dixie and let the hairstylist chop off about 8 inches of it. I hadn't cut my hair since before Grandmom's accident, so it was surprisingly emotional, but the hairstylist was gentle and sweet and did exactly what I asked for. I left about thirty minutes later feeling liberated and brand new with shoulder length, healthy hair. The shorter look suited me much better, and it stayed in a bun for diving. Cutting my hair, being inundated with beautiful reefscapes and saltwater wildlife, and the generally Zen atmosphere of the Keys all collaborated into a healing salve for my exhausted heart, and I fell quietly and madly in love with island life. By the time we left the islands we'd logged two weeks' worth of dives, swam with Barracuda as big as a full-grown man, countless beautiful reef fish, several reef sharks, and a pair of majestic Spotted Eagle Rays. I was a revived and fresh version of myself, and my heart felt three tons lighter than it had since February 2014.

Bahamas

The Keys trip ended, we came home, and I was immediately homesick for the mangroves and the rainbow-colored reefs. I waited for the homesickness to fade for months, but it never did. I'd only ever felt homesick for Pensacola, so feeling that way for a place I'd been in for a mere two weeks felt fake and dramatic. I tried to put it out of my mind, but every night when I closed my eyes, I sank into dreams about flying over purple sea fans and making friends with parrot fish. About six months after the trip, Christmas was upon us. Christmases post-Grandmom are still not normal, but those first few years were impossibly painful and felt like one gigantic slap in the face from my grief. While I was driving up to Mom and Dad's house a few days before Christmas Eve and crying to Michael Bublé's annual Christmas album, reminiscing on the Keys trip for the thousandth time, and suddenly a voice in my head screamed "LEAVE!" I yelped in surprise, immediately turned down the radio and stopped crying, and pulled over to the side of the road.

"Leave? Leave where? Or what?" I thought out loud.

"Just go," said my brain.

It occurred to me that it was entirely possible I was having a mental breakdown at this point, but I decided to roll with it. I was tired of feeling sad and numb and at least a mental breakdown would be interesting.

"Go where? Pensacola is home," I said to the voice in my head. *"Just go,"* said my brain.

Well okay. As vague as this new idea was, it prompted me to reconsider the definition of 'home' for what felt like the millionth time in my life. I had never felt at home in Mississippi, defaulting more to Pensacola. Then I remembered how at home I'd felt horseback riding, and again since I'd moved to Pensacola, and again in the Keys. It occurred to me suddenly that maybe 'home' didn't have to refer to a singular place. Then I spiraled into a black hole of thought. Maybe home was a lot of places. Maybe it really only applied to a feeling and it wasn't a place at all. What if there were a lot of places I'd feel at home in? What if I hadn't actually found home yet, just places I really liked? Underwater was certainly toward the top of the list but technology hasn't made it possible to live there yet, so moving to an actual coral reef wasn't an option. I took a deep breath and tried to clear my head.

"Go find home," said my brain as I exhaled. *"Find your joy."*

Find my joy. It had been a very long time since I'd felt anything I could label as true joy other than while diving. Under the water, I had no problem feeling every emotion the water threw my way. I laughed freely and I cried often, and it felt good to emote under water. On the surface, though, too much feeling was a threat to the control I so desperately clung to. Finding my joy was a foreign but enticing concept. I took a deep breath, decided to just survive Christmas, then revisit this whole revelation after the holidays. I shoved down the feelings again, turned the radio back on, and pulled back onto the highway.

I got through the holidays and managed to enjoy myself more than I was sad, which was a huge success compared to the prior two Christmases. When I got home to Pensacola, I remembered the conversation I'd had with myself on the trip to Mom and Dad's and started to ponder the concept of 'home' again. Since the day I was old enough to understand the concept of traveling, I've always wanted to see everywhere. Wanderlust runs through my veins at a higher concentration than oxygen, much to Mom's dismay. Over the next few weeks I toyed with the idea of maybe moving somewhere else. I had gotten comfy with the idea that Pensacola would always be home, but I did know that didn't mean I couldn't live in other places too. I started researching, looking into tropical locations that would offer plenty of diving.

Quickly I realized moving to another country could get expensive really quickly and involved a lot of paperwork. I decided if I were going to dedicate that level of energy and attention to this project, I needed to go somewhere I could be happy staying for a long time. I looked into moving to the Keys and didn't cross it off the list but decided something less familiar and expensive might be fun too. Costa Rica, Fiji, Guam, and Puerto Rico all flooded my search pages. I soon found that Costa Rica is wildly difficult to move to, so I crossed it off the list and decided to just plan to visit instead. Fiji and Guam felt a little bit far away for a permanent residence, so I crossed them off too. Puerto Rico seemed doable, but at that point the idea of being fully immersed in Spanish, despite having gotten my degree in it, was intimidating. Anxiety crossed that one off for me. Then I remembered the Bahamas.

I pulled up page after page of info on moving from the U.S. to a

Bahamian island. I knew I didn't want to be in Nassau, having had

my fill of tourism culture in Pensacola, but the idea of a remote

island was very appealing. I dove headfirst into learning everything

I could about the Bahamas and comparing each livable island. By

March, I'd narrowed it down to a few islands and printed out the

paperwork and to-do lists I needed to move myself and Scruffy to a

Bahama. I didn't tell a soul what I was doing. I didn't want to jinx it

or stress anyone out, especially if it ended up not happening. I'd

been joking about running away to the Bahamas for years, so I knew

people might not take it seriously anyway and opted to save myself

from that backlash. By day, I went about my daily life, going to work

and making memories with my friends. By night, I was filling out

paperwork and gathering documents. When I slept, I dreamt of

living in a small beach house with Scruffy, waking up to the tropical

sunrises, snorkeling and diving in my front yard all day, and falling

asleep to the sound of the waves. Then in August, everything

changed.

I'm on the manta again, but this time she's slowly skimming the surface and I'm gazing into the sky. It's exploding in an array of violent purples, oranges, reds, golds, blues, and in some areas even greens. The glowing clouds streak across the sky as though they've just been painted by an artist's brush. Every color sings a different tune, and they're echoing a melancholy song in my ears. My heart is breaking as I stare at the display above the horizon, but I don't know why. I long to stretch my arms and fly amongst the clouds, to drag my fingertips through the intense colors and spread my own paint into the mix. The ray flaps her wings slowly and smoothly in time with the sad music and we glide through the water barely disturbing the surface. I notice the sunset is reflected in the water around us, a rippling mirror of the sky. I reach out and dip my fingers into a bright streak of gold, and they're coated in sparkling paint. The ray stops, lets herself settle on the surface, and stretches out her wings, making her back flat like a canvas. I reach down and spread the gold across the top of her head like a crown and she purrs. I stretch out and dip my fingertips into some purple clouds reflected across the waves, then spread them across her left wing. Then blue. Then deep reds and bright oranges. While I paint, I sing with the sunset song. I don't understand the words, but they make me lonely. When I finish painting, there's a bold, colorful sunset finger-painted onto the ray's back. The waves don't wash it off and she's purring with delight. I move back to give her space, and she dives down into the dark water, glowing as she moves away. I float on my back and gaze up into the deepening colors of the sky, and drift to sleep as I wake up.

Kevin

ding

I became aware of the sunlight on my face and simultaneously hated it and my phone for waking me up. I was off that day, and I was determined to sleep in. I grumbled, snuggled down deeper under my thick, teal comforter. I had just dozed back off when it happened again.

DING. DING

"Ughhhhhh fine," I moaned to myself.

I rolled over, opened one eye, and grabbed my phone from the nightstand. I had 3 new texts in my group chat with my friends from Mississippi, Sarah and Katherine. I swiped open my screen and started reading.

Katherine: 'Rebecca. We have a proposition.'

"Sarah: 'Yeah let's do a dating app challenge! We can download an app together and see who gets a date first!'

It was clear they'd chatted about this together before texting me and I loved them for their optimism, but I was DONE dating. After

the broken engagement followed by two years of bad first dates and

getting ghosted I had officially called it quits. Besides, I was moving

to the Bahamas. I'd been on a few trips since Islamorada – Minnesota

with Josh, who'd quickly become my bestie, a few road trips around

Mississippi, and a day trip to New Orleans. I was loving the new

found sense of freedom and independence and more than ever I

didn't want a man messing that up. Quirky, forever single 'aunt'

with no kids who travels the world and randomly visits for holidays

sounded much more appealing than dating more icky boys.

Me: 'Lol sorry guys. I'm done with that. You two should do it,

though!'

Sarah: 'Awe come on! It'll be fun! Like a competition.'

Dang it, I thought. She knows how competitive I am and her

challenge unfortunately worked. I weighed the pros and cons. Cons:

human males, the risk of commitment and disrupting my Bahamian

plans. Pros: I might win, which is always fun. I could at least get a

free meal/date/drink out of it. Maybe even a dive buddy. Maybe it

wouldn't be so bad. Nobody said I had to marry the guy, after all.

Me: 'Ugh fine. Let's do it. Which app?'

Katherine: 'Yayyy!! How about OKCupid?'

Me: 'Okay cool. What are the rules?'

Katherine: 'First one to get a date wins. Don't get murdered.'

Me: 'Sweet. May the force be with you both.'

Within a week I had a dinner date planned with a guy named Kevin who used way too many emojis and exclamation points which annoyed me. Everything could *not* be that exciting. But he was Puerto Rican and spoke Spanish, and he was into Doctor Who which had recently become my new hyperfixation show, so at least we'd have something to talk about. The morning of the date I woke up with a pit of dread in my stomach. I felt nauseous and I really did NOT want to go on another first date. The repetitive monotony of "where are you from? What brought you to Pensacola? What do you do for fun?" was one of the main reasons I'd sworn off dating before this damn challenge. Halfway through the workday, I was ready to ghost Mister Exclamation Points, so I texted Jamie. I'd told her about the challenge, and I knew she'd help me settle down.

Me: 'I REALLY don't wanna go tonight. I feel sick just thinking about it.'

Jamie: 'It'll be fine!! You always go on the first date. You never know what will happen! And if it sucks you can text me and I'll get you out of it.'

That helped settle my nerves. I wasn't being kidnapped. I wasn't getting married. It was just dinner. If it was awful, I could literally just walk out and never see the guy again.

Me: 'Ugh fine. I need a drink first though. I'm a mess.'

Jamie: 'Hopjacks before your date? It's happy hour. $3 martinis.'

Me: 'PERFECT. See you there. 😊'

Several pineapple martinis later, I arrived at the restaurant early. I texted Kevin and told him I was there, and he arrived a few minutes later. I checked my makeup, let out a loud "UGHHHHHHHH" to vent my nerves, and got out of the car. He was approaching from across the parking lot.

"Hey!" he said, walking over from his car.

"Hi," I said.

"How was your class?' he asked. I mentally added to his brownie points tab for remembering a basic detail about my life.

"Good! Long. But good."

"Great! Are you hungry?"

"STARVING."

"Awesome. Let's go grab a table."

More brownie points for opening the door for me. More for letting me sit facing the door. I liked to see who came and went. After we sat down conversation started flowing pretty easily. Five hours later, I'd been laughing or smiling almost constantly the whole date. So much so that my face hurt. We realized it was late and decided to leave, so he walked me to my car (more brownie points, dammit) and asked if he could see me again. Before I could tell him no, my mouth had told him yes. I was surprised that I actually meant it. I'd had a good time, and another day of laughing sounded really good. I didn't do that enough. I got in my car, rolled my eyes, swore to myself I wouldn't get attached, texted Jamie to let her know I was alive, and drove home.

After a very successful second date at the beach, I blinked and discovered we'd been seeing each other for a few weeks. Every date still went similarly to the first one; I'd dread it, logic myself out of cancelling ("he hasn't given me any reason _not_ to go"), have a great time, then go home swearing I wouldn't get attached. Shortly after the third date, my friend Cat was throwing a birthday party for her daughter, Sam. I asked Cat if I could bring a plus one, determined to test this guy in every way imaginable if he planned on sticking around, and she agreed. The party/introducing him to my friends could not have gone better, from my perspective anyway, and I found myself relaxing around him more. Kevin fit right in with everyone I introduced him to, and I stopped having to convince myself to hang out with him. I decided it might not be so bad if we dated until I moved. At least I wouldn't be lonely, and he knew I was a project so I wasn't worried about leading him on.

About six weeks later, we were still seeing each other, and he had come over for dinner and to meet the fam, which on this night was Mom, Dad, Ben, Grandad, and Uncle Ronny. I still wasn't letting myself get emotionally attached, but in the interest of protecting myself I figured I needed to see how he jived with them. Not

surprisingly, the whole night went really well. After dinner, Kevin
and Mom were in the living room chatting. I don't remember what
they were talking about, but I remember Mom suddenly cracking up
laughing. The loud, belly laughs that come from deep down. I hadn't
heard her laugh like that since 2013 and it shook a piece of me
awake. I realized if I let Kevin stick around, I could kiss the Bahamas
goodbye. Cue the panic.

The next couple of weeks were absolute hell for me. I felt myself
getting more attached to Kevin which made me lash out and pull
away from him. I was initially shocked to discover that a part of me
was still okay with putting itself in the emotional line of fire after my
disastrous dating history, then I was mad at myself for letting him
hang around so long and for letting everyone meet him. I had
known better. Stupid, stupid, stupid. I felt trapped. I laid in bed
night after night, fighting the first battle of a war that would wage on
in my head for the next year: protect myself, or let one more person
in because he might be the real deal? Both options were scary. I
finally decided to just wait for him to screw up like they all did
eventually, then take that opportunity to cut and run.

Four months after our first date, he still hadn't screwed up. Or at six months, or eight. He kept fitting in with my friends and family and making me happy. I laughed all the time and he made me feel safe. We rarely argued, and when we did it was always calm and mature which was a refreshing change for me. Then in December 2016, his Gordito died. Kevin and his mom had been taking care of his Gordito and Gordita for years at that point, and the loss was devastating for them. The trauma of watching them go through such an intense loss triggered a lot of the feelings I'd been 'successfully' repressing for years. I knew if there was something that would push me away, this would be it. After Kevin called me with the news, I got dressed and stepped out of the house, heading to the car. I stopped on the steps and let myself consider my options for about 5 minutes.

I could get in the car, drive to the hospital, and let myself jump back into the 'grieving a grandparent' mode I still hadn't really clawed my way out of for myself. Or, I could get in the car, drive to the hospital, and be there for Kevin until the dust settled then gracefully exit the whole situation. Both scenarios were uncomfortable, but only one hurt. I suddenly realized I wasn't going anywhere. I remembered the ex-fiancée, and how even though our relationship was terrible, having him to lean on after Grandmom died helped me stay together. I remembered how good it felt to know I had people I could call no matter what time it was or how wrecked I was feeling. I remembered every moment Kevin had made me feel like my trauma wasn't a burden, and I knew I wouldn't leave. He'd been exactly what I needed, and I was shocked to find that I genuinely wanted to return the favor, so I stayed. Then I promised myself I'd start trying harder to process my own trauma so I could really start to let him in. The silly OKCupid challenge Katherine and Sarah had roped me into had worked. I was attached.

Before I knew it, we'd been together for a year and the paperwork I'd gathered for the Bahamas was collecting dust on my bookshelf. I couldn't even be mad about it. Kevin had taken my traumatized baggage in stride and gave me space when I asked for it, even though that wasn't natural for him. My depression and anxiety and PTSD didn't push him away, and he was always there to hold me if I needed it, or to listen if I didn't. I'd been with him while he grieved his Gordito, and I was starting to imagine a future with him. I still wanted to move to the Bahamas, and he wanted to come with me if I'd let him, but it didn't feel as vitally important as it had a year ago.

A month after our first anniversary, his Gordita died. I didn't think it was possible, but that loss was even more devastating for him than losing his Gordito. On the drive to his house that day, I realized this was it. I was in this relationship for the long haul. Despite my best efforts, I loved the over-excited Puerto Rican guy who made me laugh, and I knew he loved me too. As he grieved his Gordita, we discussed the future and he decided to join the Navy. It had been his dream for a long time, and I supported him wholeheartedly. Besides my relationship with the Navy via Grandad's service and my childhood in a Navy town, I knew it would provide stability for us and always keep me near an ocean so I supported his decision. That was when we knew we were in it for the long haul.

One day in March of 2018, Kevin told me his friend William needed models for a photoshoot he wanted to do. He told me to wear something nice and be ready when he got to my house to pick me up at 3pm. I knew he thought he was being sneaky, but I also knew what was really happening, so I made sure to also do my nails. He picked me up at 3pm on the dot and drove me out to Fort

Pickens, then proceeded to walk around and let William pose us for almost an hour before he finally dropped to one knee at the top of the fort. He said some romantic things sprinkled with Dragonball Z and Doctor Who references, talked about how much he loved me, and finally popped the question. I said yes, of course, grinning from ear to ear as he slid one of Grandmom's rings onto my finger. We took a few more photos with William then went to dinner at our favorite beachfront restaurant. As we ate dinner, the Blue Angels buzzed over the beach, returning home from a tour stop. The day could not have been more perfect, and we spent the rest of the week getting his business affairs tended to and talking about wedding plans. Then three days after he proposed, I kissed him goodbye and off he went to Chicago for boot camp. Our lives would never be the same.

I was standing on the shore watching the storm roll in from the south. The air tingled with electricity, and every few minutes that electricity would light up the whole sky. The wind whipped my hair around my head and screamed in my ears. The waves crashed at my feet, then ripped sand with them back into the dark water. It was raining in the distance, but the clouds around me hadn't yet gotten heavy enough to produce precipitation. I inhaled deeply. The smells of salt and freshwater collided in my nose and it thrilled me. Storms always hyped me up and made me feel strong. I inhaled deeply again, threw my head back, and yelled as loudly as I could into the whipping wind. It was cathartic, so I did it again. And again. Then it started raining. I closed my eyes and felt the water run down my face, then I looked up and was confused to see that there was no water falling from the sky. I looked down and it was definitely raining on me. My face, arms, torso, and legs had water droplets all over them, gathering and running down with gravity. But the sand next to me was dry. There was no water hitting the surface of the ocean. I gasped. It wasn't raining, I was CRYING. I let out a sob and put my hands to my face. Water was rushing out of my eyes like a sprinkler and falling all over me, but not landing on any other surface. I tried to breathe and couldn't. I tried to close my eyes and couldn't. I put my hands over my eyes and still the tears escaped, soaking my skin through my clothes. I started to panic, screaming into the wind again. Raw, guttural screams rooted in the fear that I'd never be able to stop. I was losing control over my own tears and it was terrifying. I let out one last deep, long scream, willing it to end the torture, and woke up in my bed soaked with sweat.

Nuptials

I had made a lot of emotional progress since meeting Kevin, and I was afraid that during the 8 weeks of boot camp, I'd shut down again and revert back to my old ways of shoving him away and defaulting to solitude. I knew I would never tell him any of that because I wouldn't let myself hold him back from chasing his goals, but I had nightmares about drowning most nights and worried about it almost constantly during the day. Then I got the first boot camp phone call. I was sitting on the living room floor at home when my phone rang, and I leapt to my feet and squealed when I saw the Illinois number. I answered immediately, and the moment I heard Kevin's voice I melted back to the floor, sobbing with relief. I'd missed him after all, and I was so relieved to discover that I couldn't catch my breath. Twenty minutes later, I heard the RDCs (Navy drill sergeants) yelling in the background and he had to hang up. I was walking on air for the rest of the day, though. I knew then that everything would be okay. A few short weeks later, his Mom and I met his Dad in Chicago for his graduation, and the next Monday he was back in Pensacola for his schooling and the naval influence in my life came full circle.

Immediately after he got back to Pensacola, I realized he was a very different person than the man who had proposed to me two months earlier. In bootcamp, you're trained to suppress every emotion except anger, and that had taken my sweet, doting fiancée and turned him into a brick wall of a human. I had known he'd be different, but the severity of the change was shocking. His lack of emotion toward anything plus my new resurgence of wedding-related emotions were a lot to deal with. I cried constantly. He couldn't figure out how to help me or himself, I tried not to let myself resent him, and we were both a mess for weeks. Finally, I texted my college friend, Mary, who is a therapist and also happens to be married to an ex-Marine.

Me: 'Mary, I think I'm going crazy.'

Mary: 'Why what's up?'

Me: 'I cannot stop CRYING. It's driving me nuts. I cry over everything. All the time. I've never cried like this. I didn't even think I could cry like this anymore.'

Mary: 'Well, what's happened that could be triggering that kind of response?'

Me: 'The navy LOL'

Mary: 'Ah. Yes it does that.'

Me: 'I just can't figure out WHY I'm crying. It's so constant I can't pin down a solid reason for it.'

Mary: 'How has your life changed specifically?'

Me: 'Well, Kevin is different. It's like he won't let himself be affectionate or emotional at all. Which I know happens, but it's flipped our dynamic completely inside out and it's disorienting. And the base rules are CRAP. He's not allowed to leave so we hardly get to see each other. That's really irritating after getting through the boot camp separation. Our whole life has changed and I miss the way it used to be.'

Mary: 'It sounds like you're grieving the life you guys used to have together. That's valid and normal, and you can grieve it just like we grieve big losses.'

Just like that, my brain went *click.*

It all made sense, and even more so, it all felt familiar. The way I was feeling about all of these changes was a lot like how I felt just after Grandmom died: intensely sad and wildly out of control of my own life. Realizing where all of the feelings were coming from provided the clarity I needed to take several deep breaths, focus on what was important and what was coming, and push through the feels. Kevin eventually snapped out of boot camp mode after a couple of weeks, I stopped crying over every little thing, and we got back to planning the wedding while he aced his classes. Then about four months out from his graduation and our wedding, Kevin called me:

"Hey. I have some news."

"Okay what's up?"

"My advisor just told me that in order for the Navy to move you with me to my first duty station after school, you have to be on my orders. In order for you to be on my orders, we need to be legally married about three months before I graduate."

"Oh. Okay. Wow. Okay. What do we want to do?"

"It's up to you babe. I'd marry you today if you wanted to."

"Okay let's do it. Find out what we need to do and we'll pick a date."

On June 12, 2018, we got up and got dressed for the day. I'd picked out a blue and yellow and white dress with sailboats on it at

TJ Maxx that week and he'd opted for his dress blues uniform. We stopped by Winn Dixie on the way to the courthouse and I picked out a bouquet of yellow daisies. Then we drove across town, walked into the Escambia County courthouse, made promises to each other, put on shiny new rings, signed our marriage license, posed for pictures, then drove home. It was simple. It was sweet. It was personal. It was a beautiful day. I cherish the photos of that day as much as the professional ones we'd pose for almost four months later. It was our 'paperwork' wedding, and it was perfect. It also took a LOT of stress and pressure off of our 'big' wedding and I have never regretted it.

The next few months FLEW by. Hurricane season began, which is always a bit of an upheaval in coastal areas, especially so if you're planning a wedding. We had to change our wedding date after having planned the entire thing and making several non-refundable deposits because of the Navy. Kevin kept kicking ass in school, though, and when the time came, everything pulled together beautifully. Our wedding day was October 6th, and the first week of October rolled around before we knew it. Everyone bustled about moving us into the huge beach house Mom and Dad had booked for the week and I focused on creating joyful moments for myself and the people who came to love us on our big day. As family and friends from out of town started arriving, I got more and more excited. I have a big, loud, fun family and having them all in one place to celebrate my and Kevin's joy was so exciting I could hardly stand it.

The afternoon before the wedding, Kevin and I admitted to each other we hadn't written our vows yet, so we locked ourselves in the MASSIVE closet in the master bedroom of the beach house and forced ourselves to finish them. I'd had major writer's block until then, but the minute I sat on the plush carpet and looked out the window onto the Gulf of Mexico, the words started flowing and didn't stop until I was done. I was ready. I went back downstairs and spent the rest of the day and a good part of the night hanging out with Kevin and my bridesmaids. I'd chosen the four girls who had known me longest; Hannah, Anna, Julia, and Talyr. Kevin's groomsmen were his best friend William, Hannah's husband, Patrick, Josh, who he'd gotten close with too since we met, and Ben. It was a super fun crew, and we had a great night. Eventually we all made our way to our beds, and I fell asleep as soon as my head hit the pillow, sinking into a deep, dreamless sleep.

On Wedding Day, I woke up with the sun and gazed out my bedroom window onto the beach and the emerald green water. I thought about everything that had happened to lead me here, starting with Grandad joining the Navy about sixty years before that day. I marveled at how much I had changed since moving to Pensacola and took a few minutes to bask in gratitude. Then I got up, stretched, and walked out into the main area of the house where the air was buzzing with excitement and the smell of a delicious breakfast. A few hours later, the hair girls showed up. They were doing hair and makeup for me and several of the bridesmaids, plus Mom and Cat's daughter, Sam, who was our flower girl. I knew after they finished the first styling that they were going to make us late and I started to feel anxious. By the time they finished doing all of our hair and makeup, we were two hours behind the schedule I had written up for the day and that time was eating into our photographer's time. Thankfully I'd built in some extra time in the day, but I also didn't have the braid in my hair that I had specifically requested. Everyone's hair and makeup looked fantastic, and the girls were super sweet, but I was suddenly STRESSED. Julia could tell.

Julia: "What do you need?"

Me: "I don't know. I'm just really stressed all of a sudden."

Julia: "What do you want to do?"

Me: "I want to get dressed and GO. I HATE being late."

Julia, very calmly: "Okay. Let's do it."

Her pragmatic calm was exactly what I needed. Everyone flurried around and finished getting dressed, got me into my dress and jewelry, and the next thing I knew, we were done with pictures and driving to the venue. We'd chosen a popular hotel on the beach with a perfectly green lawn between it and the sand. Several glasses of champagne and a brief floral snafu later Kevin and I were standing at the front of the crowd with our best friends and Hannah's dad making the same promises we'd made in June, but with better words, the beach in the background, and the salty breeze in our hair. We said 'I do,' took a billion more pictures, ate delicious food, and danced the night away.

Two days later, we'd had a mini-moon at the hotel and Kevin got called back to base early because Hurricane Michael was making a beeline for Pensacola. He left in a blur, I packed our stuff and drove it home, the first of many things I knew I'd do by myself while the Navy held him hostage. We'd found out a few days before the wedding where the Navy was sending us but opted to wait until after the celebration was over to tell everyone. That afternoon, I was settled back in at home and Kevin was bored in his room on base, so we decided it was time to tell everyone. Before the day was over, everyone we cared about had heard the news. We officially had three weeks to pack up our whole lives and make the cross-country move to Kitsap County, Washington; 2500 miles from home, a ferry ride from Seattle, and a whole new world.

Adventure

We'd been married for 15 whole days. Our stuff was packed and ready for the movers to pick up later that week, Kevin had graduated top of his class, we'd said goodbye to friends and family, and the car was loaded. I'd booked AirBNB's and planned our route. Our cooler was full of snacks and drinks, Scruffy's stuff was loaded up, and we were all set to start our 10-day road trip/honeymoon to Washington with lots of bucket list stops along the way. It was a trip I'd always dreamed of taking. I should have been excited, but the night before we left I was lying in bed next to my snoring husband trying not to wake him up while I cried. I was going to miss Pensacola, but even more, I desperately missed Grandmom. I had lived in her house for years and dreamed about her often, during that time. I had hoped for a dream during our wedding week but hadn't gotten one. That hurt as much as moving across the country from my beaches and my people.

"Please, please visit tonight. I need you. I need to talk to you before we leave. Please, please, please," I begged as I cried into my pillow. I knew it was selfish to beg her for a visit, but I was desperate. I was scared the dreams were over for good and the idea of losing that connection to her was too much to bear. I begged for a dream over and over until I finally cried myself to sleep.

Grandmom walked in the backdoor like she'd never left. She was wearing her red mock turtleneck and blue jeans and as I wrapped my arms around her I breathed her in deeply. She held me and let me cry for a while, then I pulled myself together and started eagerly filling her in on the last year of my life. She smiled and nodded along as I talked, but she was visibly tired and seemed to be struggling to breathe, so I walked her over to a faded yellow and white reclining lawn chair that had appeared nearby. We'd somehow moved from the house to a white void. It was silent except for us, and simultaneously comforting and off-putting. She sank onto the chair and caught her breath as I sat next to her, holding her right hand in mine just like I had years ago in her hospital room. After a few minutes, I asked her if this was her last visit. With teary, sad eyes she said, "Yeah babe. I think it is." I nodded and hugged her, and we cried together for a while. Then she kissed my head and told me she loved me, and I opened my eyes and woke up in my bedroom.

I woke up on moving day with tears on my face but smiling. The dream itself was very depressing, and I knew I'd done a bad thing begging her to visit. That's why she'd been so tired and haggard. But it was exactly what I needed, and I knew she'd been glad to see me too. A huge weight had lifted from my shoulders, and I was finally excited to get on the road. Kevin got up and we packed up the last few things, loaded us and Scruffy up in the car, and drove out of town for the last time for a long time. We had taken one last trip out to the beach the day before, but I cried a few bittersweet tears as we passed some of my other favorite places on the way out of town. The morning was emotionally tumultuous, but I knew we had a lot of adventures and fun memories ahead. We were moving to a place we'd never have chosen for ourselves, but that made it even more exciting. I was thrilled to get to see places I'd been dreaming of my whole life during our trip and getting to do it with Kevin was icing on the cake. We were leaving our home and everything we'd ever known, but for the first time in four and a half years I was voluntarily and fully excited for the future.

We spent the first night of our trip at Mom and Dad's. I was buzzing with excitement and anticipation, so I barely slept. The next morning, Mom was already gone to work when we woke up which I think was probably best. We'd said goodbye the night before and doing it in the moment might have been too overwhelming. Kevin and I were putting our stuff back in the car after breakfast and Dad snagged a moment alone with me while Kevin wrangled the suitcases. He gave me a big hug and said probably the most profound thing he's ever said to me.

"Well kiddo. I think this might be the adventure you've been waiting for. Whether you're ready or not."

Whoosh. The weight of his words hit me square in the chest and I had to look away so he wouldn't see the tears well up in my eyes.

"Yeah…I think…I think you might be right," I stammered. I hugged him hard, swallowed the lump in my throat and got into the car.

Saying goodbye to Mississippi felt hollow and distant and it was more sad recognizing that I wasn't sad about leaving Mississippi than it was actually leaving it. It hadn't really been home for a long time, if ever. I'd been forcing myself to hold onto that title for it out of obligation, but it had never really fit. The last few years of self-

discovery and healing had finally helped me sever those ties. It had

also shown me that while Pensacola would always be my favorite

place, it wasn't really home either. I breathed deeply as we crossed

the state line out of Mississippi and into our new life. I soaked in the

moment as I let myself consciously accept what I'd probably known

all along: home was never a place to begin with.

Maybe it is for some people, but I had realized that my home has

always been the people I love and the experiences that shaped me.

It's the beautiful sunsets I got to watch often from my favorite spot in

Gulf Breeze. It's good viz on a dive day and delicious food and tears

and thunderstorms and sunshine. Laughing until my stomach hurts

with my friends and cuddling with Kevin on the couch while

watching our favorite movies. It's sitting on the beach with Scruffy,

breathing in the salty air that raised me and digging my toes into the

sand that carries me no matter how far away I am.

Home is the carry-on I always take with me on my best

adventures, and now that I've found it, I'm packing it full of my favorite memories and taking it everywhere.

Epilogue

I squeezed my eyes closed and opened them again, but they refused to focus. It was our first ferry ride in Seattle, and it was dark so I couldn't see a damn thing beyond the two feet of glow surrounding the boat. *"So much for seeing Orcas today,"* I thought. The prospect of seeing a whole new ecosystem's brand of sea critters was one of the things I had immediately been excited about when we'd found out we'd be moving to the Seattle area. I was quickly discovering that orcas were much easier chased than spotted. I shook off the heavier than usual disappointment and closed my eyes. I could feel the cold air biting my cheeks and nose and hear the hull of the boat colliding with the waves. I took a deep breath and smiled - salty air. It was the first salt air I'd smelled since we'd left Pensacola three weeks before that. I took a few more deep breaths of it, ignoring how the cold air stabbed my throat on the way down. Kevin walked over to me from where he'd been standing on the opposite rail and put his arm around me from behind.

"How ya doin', babe?" he asked. It had been a hard few months and we were both feeling untethered.

I smiled and said, "Good now. I missed this smell."

He chuckled and I felt him rest his chin on my shoulder and nod. He'd always understood how connected I was to the ocean, and he knew how hard it had been for me to pack up my warm, sunny, Florida life and move to the Olympic Peninsula with him when we got married, even if the promise of adventures was alluring. Neither of us had chosen this area, but when the Navy says go, you pack your bags and leave, so here we were. It had been a week since we pulled into our new apartment's parking lot and already I was feeling the tight grip of the PNW Grey Days and desperately missing my sunshine and sugar white beaches.

Kevin hugged me tighter, equally for comfort and warmth I'm sure. We were ill prepared for the drastic drop in temperature we'd experienced moving from Florida to Washington at the end of October and our short sleeved shirts and thin jeans were providing very little warmth against the icy wind cutting across the ferry deck.

"Hey, you know this ferry ride is probably one we'll remember forever. That makes this a pretty important boat," he said.

"Ah you're right!" I realized. "We should probably know the

name of it."

I turned around and started scanning the parts of the boat I could see, looking for a nameplate. After a few seconds I spotted it, yellow letters carved into a stained wooden plank, hanging just below the windows the captain looked out of.

"*Kaleetan.* I need to look that one up," I said, excited to learn the root of another of the many indigenous words used in Washington's naming systems.

I took another deep breath of the frigid salt air, closed my eyes again, and let the rocking of the ferry lull me into warmer memories of other very important boats.

Acknowledgements

I've been 'writing' this book in my head since I learned how to talk, but I didn't start actually writing down any of those thoughts until Spring 2019. For five and a half years I cried, laughed, cursed, and sometimes drank my way through pulling these memories out of my head and spewing them into a word document. A huge thank you to the people who watched and listened while I shaped it all into a book. Your support means the world to me.

To my proofreaders, editors, and beta readers - you all keep me sane. Thank you for your input and honesty.

To my writer friends, Katherine and Julia – thank you both for your guidance and encouragement. It took a while, but I wouldn't have finished this without you.

To Emma – thank you for being a steady sounding board and a safe place to finish my first draft. And for drinking champagne with me after I realized it was finished.

To Dad – thank you for being the force of adventure behind many of these memories and for always encouraging me to go see the world (safely, of course). I love ya, Pops.

To Ben – the calm to my storm. You're my first best friend and I'm so glad I got to grow up with you. I love you, Buzz.
To Mom – thank you for teaching me to love words and books, and for being as nostalgic as I am. Thank you for being my beach buddy and for giving me the gift of horses. Thank you for teaching me to believe in myself. This one's for us. I love you.

To Kevin, my steady partner and my love - thank you for always listening to me read aloud when I needed to, for holding me when some memories got hard to remember, and for being my encouragement when I needed a push to keep going. You're my favorite decision I continue to make. I love you forever.